~Introducing Theology Series~
Vol.1

Introducing *the* Early *Kalam* Controversies

Course Notes

Written and compiled by

SAFARUK Z. CHOWDHURY

AD-DUHA
LONDON 2009

©Ad-Duha, London 2012

First edition 2008

Updated Edition 2012

An educational publication from Ad-Duha London
Third Floor, 42 Fieldgate Street
London E1 1ES
E: info@duha.org.uk
W: www.duha.org.uk
T: 07891 421 925

TABLE OF ABBREVIATIONS

Art.	= article
Bk.	= book
pp.	= pages
ʾ	= the Arabic letter ع
ʿ	= the Arabic letter ء
اهـ	= 'end of quote' where a cited textual segment in Arabic ends.
s:	= additional comments made by the translator

TABLE OF SYMBOLS

§	= *hadith* number
(…)	= contains transliteration of Arabic terms
[…]	= contains additions by the translator
… / […]	= ellipsis where a textual segment is elided and omitted in translation by the translator
{...}	= enclosure of a Qurʾanic verse in translation
§	= section

CONTENTS PAGE

Topics	Page

Part 1: Introducing the *Kalam* Controversy   7-36

1. Atoms, Bodies and Accidents.
2. Rationalist Presuppositions.
3. Scripturalist Presuppositions.
4. Early Crucibles for Theological Divergences.
5. The Method of the *Mutakallimun*.
6. al-Barbahari's Censure of *Kalam*.
7. al-Ash'ari's Vindication of *Kalam*.
8. Two Examples of Hanbalite Scholars using *Kalam*.

Part 2: The Created Qur'an Controversy   38-50

1. Presuppositions of the Controversy.
2. Key words in the Controversy.
3. Different Views on Qur'an being created.
4. A Summary of both Scripturalist and Rationalist Views.
5. Two early Muslim Creeds: IbnKhuzaymah and al-Isfara'ini.

Part 3: The Divine Attributes Controversy   52-88

1. The Controversy: Theological Backdrop.
2. Understanding the problem of divine attributes: Ibn al-Jawzi.
3. Understanding the Arabic Language.
4. *Ta'wil*.
5. Examples of *Ta'wil* by Early Muslims.
6. A Unified Creed: al-Ash'ari.

Part 4: The Freewill Controversy   90-114

1. Hellenistic Background.
A. Part 1: Origins of the Controversy.
B. Part 2: Meaning of the Terms *Qada'* and *Qadar*.
C. Part 3: Revisiting *Qada'* and *Qadar*.
D. Part 4: *Qada'* and *Qadar*: Conclusions.
E. Part 5: al-Ash'ari and the Theory of *Kasb*.

Bibliography   115

Introduction

This booklet comprises of the notes accompanying the course *Early Kalam Controversies* delivered to undergraduate students for the 'Islamic Theology and Philosophy' module 2008-2010. It introduces some of the key theological debates within the early Muslim intellectual community that have relevance and has as much intensity today as they did historically. The causes and presuppositons surrounding the controversies are outlined and given focus with ample textual examples from the formative period of Islam. The notes are marginally referenced and are terse in many places assuming some prior familiarity with the literature gained from reading during the term. The booklet serves as primary reading material for the lectures and so all references ought to be followed up in discussions whether in class or in separate study circles.

S. Z. C.
London, 2012.

Part One: Kalam

1) Atoms, Bodies and Accidents.
2) Rationalist Presuppositions.
3) Scripturalist Presuppositions.
4) Early Crucibles for Theological Divergences.
5) The Method of the *Mutakallimun*.
6) al-Barbahari's Censure of *Kalam*.
7) al-Ash'ari's Vindication of *Kalam*.
8) Two Examples of Hanbalite Scholars using of Kalam.

"Atoms, Bodies and Accidents:
Introducing the Universe of the Mutakallimun"

Course Module: 'Early Islamic Controversies'.
Topic: *the mutakallim's ontology*.
Instructor: S. Z. Chowdhury
Venue: ad-Duha Institute, London.

---

§1. The 'stuff' of reality:

- The practitioners of *kalam*, especially the Ash'arite theologians, have outlined what things *exist*. In philosophy, this is called *ontology* (Greek: ὄντος) or the philosophical study pertaining to being, existence and reality and how they can be grouped.

- Put simply, there is first Allah and *then everything else*. The 'everything else other than Allah' category of things can be delineated as follows:

Atoms/substance (*jawhar*)	Accidents (*'arad*)[1]	Bodies (*jism*)
1. That which occupies space, i.e. extended in space.	1. That which inheres in an object.	1. Assemblage of atoms/substances.
2. That which is finitely divisible into parts.	2. A contingent property.	2. A 'lattice' of atoms and there accidents.
3. An isolated entity.	3. Something that persists for a finite duration.	3. A composite entity.
4. That which exists.	4. A change that qualifies an atom or substance.	
5. Smallest unit of matter.		

---

[1] The term *'arad* is Qur'anic in origin and form but not in the sense given to it by the philosophers and *mutakallimun*. || See τό συμβεβηκός from Aristotle's *Metaphysics* 1025a14.

General references: R. M. Frank, "The Ash'arite Ontology: I: Primary Entities", *Arabic Sciences and Philosophy* 9, Cambridge, 1999, pp.163-231, idem "Bodies and Atoms: The Ash'arite Analysis" in *Islamic Theology and Philosophy*, ed. M. Marmura, pp.39-53; A. Sabra, "Kalam Atomism as An alternative Philosophy to Hellenizing *Falsafa*" in *Arabic Theology, Arabic Philosophy*, ed. by J. E. Montgomery, pp.199-273 and A. Dhanani, *The Physical Theory of Kalam*, pp.15-90.

"Rationalist Presuppositions"

Course Module: 'Early Islamic Controversies'.
Topic: *rationalist presuppositions*.
Instructor: S. Z. Chowdhury
Venue: ad-Duha Institute, London.

———◆———

	Area of theology	View	Justification
[1]	Reason (*'aql*)	1] required to understand text (scripture); 2] necessary to establish, articulate and formulate foundations for theological beliefs/doctrines; 3] can be used to qualify and restrict text; 4] fallible; 5] used for metaphysical enquiry and logic as a formal area of enquiry; 6] the natural world is amenable to rational investigation and study; 7] can be used to establish the existence of God and the contingency of the cosmos/temporal world; 8] used to formulate rational principles; 9] used to understand Allah's attributes and their implications; 10] it can intuit values or moral properties;	1] reason does not lead to heresy but certainty; only blind following and ignorance leads to heresy; 2] reason is *chronologically* prior to faith and revelation and hence primary and so to discard it is dangerous and foolish; 3] reason complements and strengthens revelation – it is the *handmaiden* of revelation not its enemy; 4] reason is not divisive but enlightening and elevating; 5] reason is stable whereas tradition and homogeneity can be unstable; 6] making *ta'wil* ('figurative interpretation of scripture') is necessary which obviates any tendencies or routes to anthropomorphism and andropomorphism; 7] dispensing with reason makes a mockery of apologetics and polemics with other traditions;
[2]	Homogeneity	1] necessary; 2] disagreements are equated with positivity and diversity or dynamism; 3] it i is not forbidden to oppose all forms of consensus (*ijma'*); 4]	1] The philosophers and *kalam* scholars use coherent rational and intellectual principles; 2] difference amongst the philosophers and *kalam* scholars

		debates (*jadal*) and argumentation are healthy and this dialectic helps refine thinking and conclusions and does not undermine homogeneity; 5] protects and safeguards from heresy and innovation; 6] principles of the religion are unchanging;	indicate their rich intellectual foundations and vibrancy as well as their desire for truth; 3] they were also prone to heresy because they lacked correct understanding, application, uniformity and homogeneity
[3]	Early generation (*al-salaf*)	1] the *sahaba* preserved and transmitted the religion; 2] the pious community (*salaf*) codified and embodied a living tradition of Islam; 3] the practitioners and critics of *hadith* must be respected but are not the only group to embody the entire tradition; 4] their legal derivations are equal to any other legal derivation;	1] rejection of the *sahaba* undermines the religion itself; 2] the early community are the praised generations and hence the main vehicle through which the religion was understood and lived and rejection of it is in essence a rejection of the living tradition;
[4]	Traditions (*ahadith*)	1] A foundation of the religion and Law; 2] used to interpret theological claims and beliefs; 3] a source and criterion of truth claims about reality; 4] all types are affirmed for grounding law and doctrine; 5] differentiation in degree or levels of *hadith*;	1] epistemological distinctions in *hadith* grades (*ahad* vs. *mutawatir*) that are warranted; 2] traditions that contradict what is rationally certain may be put aside;
[5]	Consensus (*ijma'*)	1] an independent proof in itself; 2] all types are not necessarily upheld; 3] can be dispensed with; 4] may not necessarily be a criterion of truth;	

Basic References: O. Leaman, *An Introduction to Classical Islamic Philosophy*, pp.1-49; A. S. Tritton, "Reason and Revelation" in *Arabic and Islamic Studies in Honour of Hamilton A. R. Gibb*, ed. by G. Makdisi, pp.619-631; G. F. Hourani, *Reason and Tradition in Islamic*

Ethic, pp.6-14; J. Walbridge, *God and Logic in Islam*, pp.9-54 and B. Abrahamov, *Islamic Theology*, pp.32-48.

"Scripturalist Presuppositions"

Course Module: 'Early Islamic Controversies'.
Topic: *scripturalist presuppositions*.
Instructor: S. Z. Chowdhury
Venue: ad-Duha Institute, London.

———◆———

	Area of theology	View	Justification
[1]	Reason (*'aql*)	1] subordinated to text (scripture); 2] cannot be used to formulate foundations for theological beliefs/doctrines; 3] cannot be used to oppose text; 4] fallible; 5] no place for metaphysics or logic as a formal area of enquiry; 6] *bi-la kayfah* ('without modality') doctrine;	1] reason leads to heresy and hence must be restricted; 2] reason is *salvifically* posterior to faith and revelation and hence secondary; 3] reason obviates the need for revelation as people will rely on reason and this is absurd; 4] reason is divisive, i.e. it splits up the community of believers; 5] reason is unstable whereas tradition and homogeneity are stable; 6] rejection of *ta'wil* ('figurative interpretation of scripture') because it leads to distortion and in the end denial of scriptural statements;
[2]	Homogeneity	1] obligatory and necessary; 2] disagreements are equated with sectarianism; 3] forbidden to oppose all forms of consensus (*ijma'*); 4] debates (*jadal*) and argumentation endanger homogeneity and thus are forbidden; 5] protects and safeguards from heresy and innovation; 6] principles of the religion are unchanging;	1] The philosophers and *kalam* scholars always change their mind and thus are unstable and incoherent; 2] difference amongst the philosophers and *kalam* scholars indicate their lack of intellectual foundations and coherence; 3] they were also prone to heresy because they lacked uniformity and homogeneity
[3]	Early generation (*al-*	1] the *sahaba* preserved and	1] rejection of the *sahaba*

	salaf)	transmitted the religion; 2] the pious community (*salaf*) codified and embodied a living tradition of Islam; 3] the practitioners and critics of *hadith* must be venerated;	undermines the religion itself; 2] the early community are the praised generations and hence the vehicle through which the religion was understood and lived and rejection of it is in essence a rejection of the living tradition;
[4]	Traditions (*ahadith*)	1] A Foundation of the religion and law; 2] used to interpret theological claims and beliefs; 3] a source and criterion of truth claims about reality; 4] all types are affirmed for grounding law and doctrine; 5] no differentiation in degree or levels of *hadith*;	1] rationalists invented epistemological distinctions in *hadith* grades that are totally unwarranted;
[5]	Consensus (*ijma'*)	1] an independent proof in itself; 2] all types are upheld; 3] cannot be dispensed with; 4] a criterion of truth;	

Basic References: O. Leaman, *An Introduction to Classical Islamic Philosophy*, pp.1-49; A. S. Tritton, "Reason and Revelation" in *Arabic and Islamic Studies in Honour of Hamilton A. R. Gibb*, ed. by G. Makdisi, pp.619-631; G. F. Hourani, *Reason and Tradition in Islamic Ethic*, pp.6-14; J. Walbridge, *God and Logic in Islam*, pp.9-54 and B. Abrahamov, *Islamic Theology*, pp.1-32.

"Early Crucibles for Theological Divergences"

Course Module: 'Early Islamic Controversies'.
Topic: *historical context*
Instructor: S. Z. Chowdhury
Venue: ad-Duha Institute, London.

───────◆───────

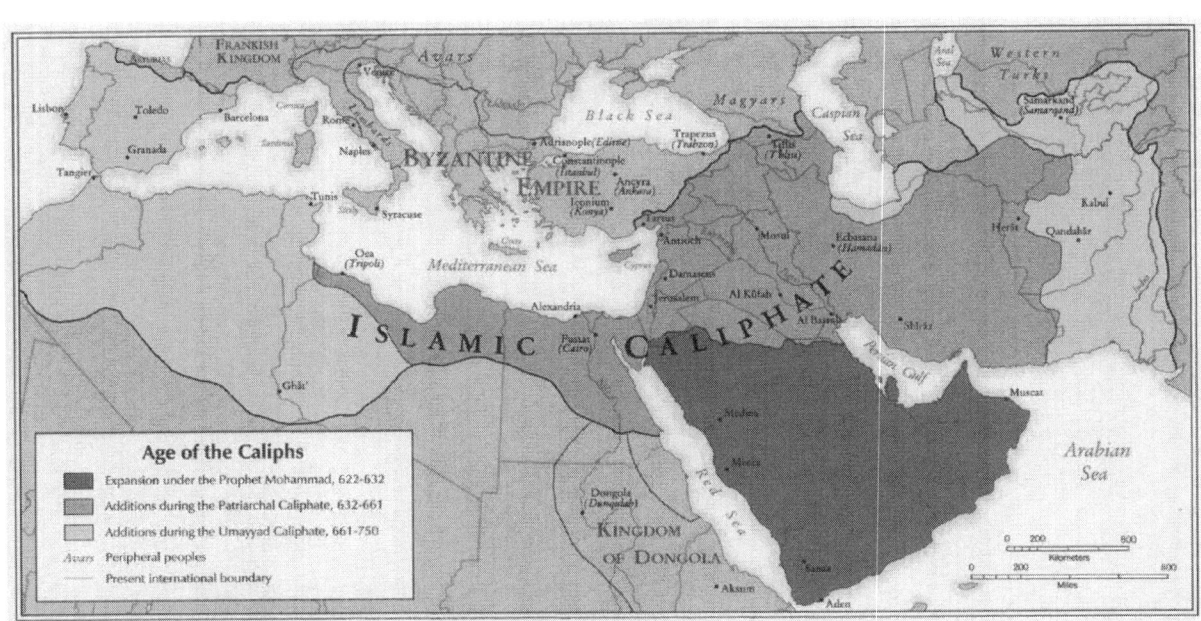

Four groups emerged in early Islamic history that became the pretext for later theological schisms within the Muslim community. The traumatic upheaval of 24 / 656 AD which marked the assassination of 'Uthman Ibn 'Affan (r. 644-656) led to the most evident fracture of the Muslim community and laid down the foundations of many subsequent sectarian alignments – this political fracture was termed the *fitnah* ('the great schism').

'A'ishah (Sunnism I)	Mu'awiyah (Sunnism II)	'Ali (Shi'ite)	Khawarij
Battle of the camel (656) near Basra where Ali's forces met 'A'ishah's in hope of clearing up the cause behind the	Battle of Siffin (657) between 'Ali's forces and Mu'awiyah's army with Mu'awiyah's vigour and acumen later	Legitimate fourth Muslim Caliph but faced dissention from all sides; his supporters became the proto-Shi'ite	An extremist dissenting faction from amongst Ali's supporters and later became the origin of theological

| assassination of 'Uthman; | restoring Muslim political unity (661-662) inaugurating the Umayyad political clan; | predecessors; | controversies surrounding free will and belief; |

 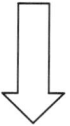 

Proto-Sunni Beliefs

- Deterministic in tendency – but in the political context;

- A ruler is fated to be so and thus such an idea is congenial to legitimising the rulers because it diminishes concern for the morality of their actions;

- Determinism appears to also ground the exalted power of God and thus theologically positive whereas an underscored and emphasised view of human free will and agency undermined Divine authority over creation (cf. 'Umar Ibn 'Abd al-Aziz);

- A pietistic trend on upholding free will (*qadariyyah*) was however absorbed by proto-*sunni* and hadith scholars;

Beliefs

A ruler must be a descendant of the Prophet;

No elections for political successors;

Sinners are not non-Muslims;

A deep messianic impulse underpinned Shi'ite religious activity and paved the way for Isma'ili "*da'wa*" and esotericism;

Beliefs

Sins of rulers meant destroyed their legitimacy and legitimised their deposition;

Committing a major sin negated faith and ex-communicated the sinner;

Their doctrine on sin led the way for discussions on human free will and responsibility (**qadarism**) upholding libertarianism (cf. Hasan al-Basri); they also became a source for later emerging theological schools like the Mu'tazilites.

By 750 AD, these four tendencies mentioned above (Sunni I & II + Shia and Kharijites) gave rise to key theological notions that formed material for later developments of distinctive theological schools and ideas in Islam. Some of these key theological schools and ideas were:

1. **Murji'ism** (refer to PPT) epitomised in Abu Hanifah (d. 767).

2. **Rationalism / Mu'tazilism** (refer to PPT) and early protagonists.

3. **Traditionism/ Scripturalism** (refer to PPT) epitomised by Ahmad Ibn Hanbal (d. 855).

4. **Ash'arism** (refer to PPT) originated by Abu 'l-Hasan al-Ash'ari (d. 936)

References: K. Blankenship, "The Early Creed" in *The Cambridge Companion to Classical Islamic Philosophy*, pp.33-54, D. Brown, *A New Introduction to Islam*, pp.172-192; A. Rippin, *Muslims: Their Religious Beliefs and Practices*, pp.59-87 and D. Waines, *An Introduction to Islam*, pp.63-103.

"Talking about *Kalam*: Definitions, Aims and Methods"

Course Module: 'Early Islamic Controversies'.
Topic: *kalam*
Instructor: S. Z. Chowdhury
Venue: ad-Duha Institute, London.

- From the Arabic root *k / l / m /* ‖ 'speech', 'talk', 'discussion', 'articulation'; from the ancient Greek "λόγος" meaning 'word', reason' and 'argument'; it is usually rendered into English as: i) speculative theology; ii) rational theology; iii) systematic theology; iv) philosophy and v) dialectics.

- Below are some meanings of the term "kalam" found in the early Muslim theological literature:

  1. *Nazar*/reflection/speculation;
  2. *Falsafah*/philosophy;
  3. *Istidlal*/inferences/reasoning;
  4. *Jadal*/*munazara*/disputation;
  5. *Ta'ammul*/thinking;

- The eastern *kalam* phase in some theological works outline the following historical developments:

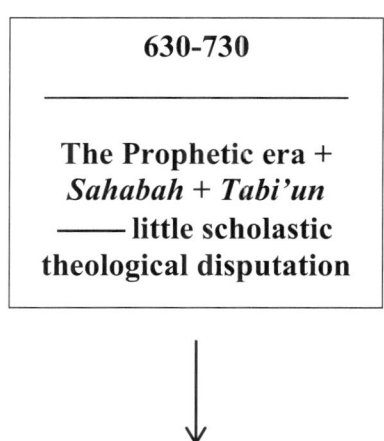

> **730-800**
>
> *A Pre Mu'tazilite 'Kalam'*: i) controversies over Qur'anic predestination (*qadar*); ii) belief (*iman*); iii) sectarian challenges, e.g. kharijite opposition + Shi'ite political opposition, etc.

> **800-950**
>
> *Development of 'Kalam'*: i) Abbasid power and relocation of Caliphate office to Iraq; ii) entry of Hellenistic thought through the translation movements iii) Muslim inter-faith polemics with Christians, Jews and Zoroastrians; iv) the rise of the Mu'tazilite and speculative theology as well as philosophy; v) *ahl al–hadith* rejection of *kalam*.

↓

> **950-1100**
>
> *Polarisation of theology*: i) *Sunnism* established through al-Ash'ari + Maturidi; ii) *Sunni* religious sciences consolidated; iii) Mu'tazilite, Ash'arite and scripturalist intra-theological polemics; iv) A decline in reception of Hellenistic philosophy although *kalam* gains impetus through Ghazali's appropriation of it.

- *Kalam* then by the 3rd / 9th and 4th / 10th centuries became a regulated scholastic science that was quite differentiated from the more abstract or 'pure' philosophy (*falsafah*) that preoccupied early figures such as al-Kindi (c. 256/870), al-Farabi and Ibn Sina although there was always overlap. It established itself as a formal discipline of intellectual inquiry, reasoning and disputation that was identified with *usul al-din* ('doctrines of Islam') and was formulated in doctrinal manuals or larger compendia with the following general schema of topics:

1. Epistemology: reason, rational inquiry and speculation.

2. Natural Theology: Proof of the existence of the Creator.

3. The attributes of this Creator – especially omniscience (knowledge), omnipotence (power) and justice.

4. Human agency and efficacy in the world (e.g. the ontological status of actions, free will and determinism, etc.).

5. The Prophethood and its veracity.

6. The afterlife.

7. Politics, e.g. governance, *Imamah*/Caliphate, etc.

- The aims of *kalam* included:

1. Establishing the intelligibility of faith.

2. Reason grounds religion.

3. The fundamental tenets of the faith are rationally demonstrable.

References: M. S. Sheikh, *Islamic Philosophy*, pp.1-31; Watt, *Islamic Philosophy and Theology*, parts 1-3, pp.1-96; Wolfson, *The Philosophy of the Kalam*, pp.1-43 and Frank, "The Science of Kalam", *Arabic Sciences and Philosophy 2*, pp.7-37.

"The Method of the *Mutakallimun*"

Course Module: 'Early Islamic Controversies'.
Topic: *method of the mutakallimun*
Instructor: S. Z. Chowdhury
Venue: ad-Duha Institute, London.

———◆———

- The *Mutakallimun* where characterised by at least three features which distinguished them from the *ahl al-hadith* or non-rationalist inclined scholars:

Theological Polemics	**Syllogistic Logic**	*Ta'wil*
[1] Debating and disputing internal Islamic religious areas like belief, God's character, Ethics, etc;	[1] Aristotelian syllogism (*qiyas*);	[1] Non-literal interpretations of Qur'anic and *hadith* references.
[2] Discussing highly theoretical and philosophical matters like metaphysics;	[2] Establishing proof (*barahin*) through syllogistic reasoning;	[2] Any interpretation of scripture or religious textual material that accords with a rational presupposition;
[3] Interfaith argumentation to prove the veracity of Islamic truth claims against for example Jews and Christians.	[3] The valid method of arriving at truth or formulating arguments are syllogisms.	

§1. Theological Polemics

Muslims were in polemical exchanges with the religious traditions that now came under their rule. These religious traditions possessed a rich intellectual history and both Christianity and Judaism had already developed theologies with Hellenistic polarisation. However, by the end of the 2nd / 8th and 3rd / 9th centuries, Muslim theology was in the ascendency with a developed system of metaphysics and polemics in the form of *kalam* and so the existing religious traditions appropriated this theological system of the *kalam* to defend against Islamic charges of irrationality. Muslim theologians and especially the *Mutakallimun* engaged in sustained debates with these other traditions as a means of missionary activity as well as to evidence the superiority of the Islamic creed over others.

Below is an excerpt from one of the earliest surviving systematic treatise on Muslim polemics by the Ash'arite theologian Abu Bakr al-Baqlillani (d. 403/1013) on rejecting the union of the divine Word with that of Christ's body which is a favourite polemical topos even for contemporary Muslim missionaries (see: *Kitab al-Tamhid*, para. 40-41 = D. Thomas edn. in *Christian Doctrines in Islamic Theology*, pp.93-195 and para.174-175, pp.98-99 of R. J. McCarthy from MSS Bibliothèque Nationale arabe 6090; Aya Sophia 2201 and 'Atif Efendi 1223).

١٧٤ و" "يقال لهم: لم قلتم إن كلمة الله اتحدت بجسد المسيح دون جسد موسى وإبراهيم وغيرهما من النبيّين؟ فإن قالوا: لأجل ما ظهر على يد عيسى من فعل الآيات واختراع المعجزات التي لا يقدر البشر على مثلها، من نحو إحياء الموتى وإبراء الأكمه والأبرص وجعل القليل كثيراً وقلب (ص٩٥ظ) الماء خمراً والمشي على الماء وصعوده السماء وإبراء الزمن وإقامة المقعد وغير ذلك من عجيب الآيات. فوجب أنه إله وأن الكلمة متحدة به. يقال لهم: لم زعمتم أن عيسى فاعل لم وصفتم من الآيات ومخترع لها؟ وما أنكرتم أن يكون غيره قادر على قليل من ذلك ولا كثير، وأن يكون الله تعالى هو الذي (ف ٦٦ و) فعل جميع ما ظهر على يده من ذلك، وتكون حاله فيه حال (ب ٣٠ و) سائر الأنبياء. فيا ظهر عليهم من الآيات؟

١٧٥ ثم يقال لهم: فلِم أنكرتم أن يكون موسى عليه السلام إلها؟ وأن تكون الكلمة متحدة به لما فعله من الآيات البديعة، نحو قلب العصا حيّة ذات فم وعينين وخروق - ولم تكن من قبل حيّة ولا فيها رسم عين ولا فم - ونحو فلق البحر وإخراج يده بيضاء. وغير ذلك، وما أتى به من الجراد والقمّل والضفادع والدم وغير ذلك مما لا يقدر عليه البشر؟

Christian:

[P1] No human is able to give life to the dead, heal the blind, make what is little a lot, turn water into wine, walk on water, etc.

[C] *Therefore*, it must be that Christ must be Divine (*ilah*) and the Word united with him

Baqillani:

[P1] Moses turned a staff into a serpent with a mouth and organs, fully parted the sea, withdrew a glowing hand, etc.
[P2] These actions cannot be performed by humans;

_____

[C] *Therefore*, it must be that Moses must be Divine and possible for the Word to unite with him.

Problems:

1. The Muslim polemics often took place within extremely intricate and theoretical matters divorced from simpler and more austere discussions; this often led to abstract and dry books being written or theological hair-splitting and subsidiary issues of definitions and ramifications.

2. Often the discussion centred on God, Divine attributes and abstract matters and framed within a *kalam* metaphysics (substance, atoms, accidents…); this was not necessarily always helpful and produced lengthy discussions on areas of speculation that failed to produce definitive rational judgements because they were in effect beyond sense-perception.

§2. Syllogistic Logic

The general early entry of Aristotelian philosophy and its subsequent reception into 2nd / 8th and 3rd / 9th century Islamic philosophical formulations and *kalam* discourse was far-reaching. Aristotle's *Metaphysics*, *Topics*, *Prior Analytics* and *Posterior Analytics* as well as his *Organon* were thoroughly translated into Arabic and found commentaries and expansions by notable philosophers such as al-Farabi (d. 339/950) and Ibn Sina (d. 428/1037) who developed their own systems of logic. With the flowering of *sunni* theology in the form of Ash'arism after the late 4th / 10th century and its subsequent triumph over Mu'tazilite rationalism, syllogistic logic (*qiyas*) was thoroughly appropriated as an attractive intellectual tool within Islamic monotheistic polemics and theological study with even claims of Qur'anic proofs for its vindication (cf. S. Z. Chowdhury, "Greek Logic and Qur'anic Arguments: A Medieval Islamic Merger", MA thesis, SOAS 2006).

Basic Aristotelian terms for a categorical syllogism which comprises of two premises and one conclusion are:

Premises	= *muqaddimat*; these are the statements of an argument within a syllogism
Major Premise	= *muqaddimat al-kubra*; this is some general statement or claim usually assumed to be true
Minor Premise	= *muqaddimat al-sughra*; usually a more specific statement as is also assumed to be true
Major term	= *hadd al-akbar*; this is a word found in the major premise that becomes the predicate of the conclusion
Minor term	= *hadd al-asghar*; this is a word found in the minor premise that becomes the subject of the conclusion
Middle term	= *hadd al-awsat*; the term found in both the major and minor premises
Figure	= *shakl*; this is the form of the syllogism which depends on whether the middle term is a subject or predicate in a specific premise.
Conclusion	= *natijah*; this is the result from the two premises and may not always be

Examples:

(1)

[P1] All Mu'taziltes were rationalists.
[P2] Some Ash'arites were Mu'tazilites.

[C] *Therefore*, Some Ash'arites were rationalists

(2)

[P1] No Mutakallim was an Ahl al-Hadith.
[P2] All Rationalists were a Mutakallim.

[C] *Therefore*, No Rationalist was an Ahl-Hadith

Below is an excerpt from one of the most vehement opponents of Greek logic in Islamic medieval polemic Ibn Taymiyyah (d. 728/1328). He sought to undermine logic as a sound system of reasoning and composed a treatise entitled *al-Radd 'ala 'l-Mantiqiyyin* and abridged as *Jahd al-Qarihah fi Tajrid al-Nasihah* by Jalal al-Din al-Suyuti (translated by W. Hallaq in *Ibn Taymiyya Against the Greek Logicians*, pp.6-174 and cf. *Majmu' al-Fatawa*, vol. ix below). Ibn Taymiyyah is arguing that the non-existent consideration given to logic by scholars of Islam through all early generations is an indication it was never needed. He also argues that logic offers no practical benefits or usefulness – especially in ethical, political and social contexts. This he argues men learn from trial and error, experiences and sensation of the reality:

وأيضا لا تجد أحدا من أهل الأرض حقق علما من العلوم وصار إماما فيه مستعينا بصناعة المنطق لا من العلوم الدينية ولا غيرها فالأطباء والحساب والكتاب ونحوهم يحققون ما يحققون من علومهم وصناعاتهم بغير صناعة المنطق . وقد صنف في الإسلام علوم النحو واللغة والعروض والفقه وأصوله والكلام وغير ذلك . وليس في أئمة هذه الفنون من كان يلتفت إلى المنطق بل عامتهم كانوا قبل أن يعرب هذا المنطق اليوناني . وأما العلوم الموروثة عن الأنبياء صرفا وإن كان الفقه وأصوله متصلا بذلك فهي أجل وأعظم من أن يظن أن لأهلها التفات إلى المنطق إذ ليس في القرون الثلاثة من هذه الأمة – التي هي خير أمة أخرجت للناس – وأفضلها القرون الثلاثة : من كان يلتفت إلى المنطق أو يعرج عليه مع أنهم في تحقيق العلوم وكمالها بالغاية التي لا يدرك أحد شأوها كانوا أعمق الناس علما وأقلهم تكلفا وأبرهم قلوبا

"As well, we do not find a single person on the face of the earth – whether specialised in a particular science or became an Imam – who was helped by logic; neither in worldly matters or other than it. Doctors, Mathematicians, writers and people like them who have become specialists in their respective disciplines or professions did so without logic. Moreover, in Islamic books on grammar, linguistics, *fiqh* and its principles as well as theology were all composed and none of the scholars in these sciences turned to logic; rather many of them were around before Greek logical treatises were translated in to Arabic […]".

Problems:

1. To claim that syllogistic logic is the *only* means to certainty or certain truth inevitably undermines the efficaciousness of the era of the Prophet and his companions as they arrived at the certainties of faith (*iman*) without the process of moving from a major premise, minor premise and then its conclusion, i.e. salvation would have to rest on mastering the art of the syllogism. This would therefore entail all Muslims would be in need of learning Aristotelian syllogisms to earn Divine salvation. This contradicts scripture.

2. This strict insistence that rational proof, definitive judgements and certainties is only attainable through deductive reasoning in the form of Aristotelian syllogisms also opposes Qur'anic mode of intellectual inquiry which is mainly reasoning from

perceptible data that appeals to a natural form of inductive and *a fortiori* reasoning without logical particulars.

3. Deductive logic in the form of the valid figures of a syllogism yields valid conclusions; nevertheless this does not mean the premises are actually true (look at the syllogism examples above). The only way to know if one of the premises are true is through sense perception, i.e. whether it is grounded in reality and not abstract theoretical postulation or assumption. Much of the *kalam* speculative reasoning rested on first hypothesising or postulating a set of claims and then formulating the argument into a syllogistic figure without ascertaining whether the postulated claim was established empirically.

§3. *Ta'wil*

[For details, refer to the *ta'wil* section below]

If reason takes primacy in arbitrating the veracity of a particular claim, especially regarding the divine attributes, then the Qur'anic text was no exception. The desire to maintain Allah's transcendence (*tanzih*) was paramount for both scripturalist theologians and rationalist theologians. However, rationalist theologians like the Mu'tazilites approached scriptural references to what appear to be surface anthropomorphic ascriptions with total negation and gave metaphorical glosses (*ta'wil*) to them. It was inconceivable to the mind that scripture intend physical attributes for Allah so they were not taken literally and denied attribution to Him. Thus, contravention of reason was the justification to reject the apparent surface meanings of the Qur'an.

Problems:

1. *Ta'wil* was not a practice of the Prophet or his Companions as they did not see any issue or matter that needed to be reconciled, fixed or addressed with regards to Qur'anic meanings and implications or contradictions between reason and revelation.

2. There is no essential need to investigate the verses of the Qur'an that contain ambiguous statements as this could lead to confusion and even outright heresy.

3. Why must the Qur'anic text conform to a priori standards of the mind (*'aql*) because it is not clear why the mind should be what decides whether a verse is taken with a specific meaning or not.

References: H. Abdul-Raof, *Theological Approaches to Qur'anic Exegesis*, pp.29-37; al-Nabhani, *al-Shakhsiyyah al-Islamiyyah*, vol.1, pp.49-65; J. Lameer, *al-Farabi and Aristotelian Syllogistics*, pp.40-97 and T. Street, "Arabic Logic" in *Greek, Indian and Arabic Logic*, ed. by Gabbay et al, pp.527-593.

"Never the Twain shall Meet: al-Barbahari's Censure of *Kalam*"

Course Module: 'Early Islamic Controversies'.
Topic: *censure of kalam*.
Instructor: S. Z. Chowdhury
Venue: ad-Duha Institute, London.

———◆———

- Below are excerpts from the book *Sharh al-Sunnah* attributed to the firebrand cleric al-Barbahari (d. 329/941) who was one of the foremost theologians in Iraq belonging to the Hanbalite School. He was known for his militant criticisms of *kalam* and its methods. It was this vitriolic attack on rational or scholastic theology that led al-Ash'ari to produce a response vindicating *kalam* especially in that the attack implicated him:

Para. 8:

واعلم رحمك الله أنه ليس في السنة قياس ولا تضرب لها الأمثال ولا تتبع فيها الأهواء بل هو التصديق بآثار رسول الله صلى الله عليه وسلم بلا كيف ولا شرح ولا يقال لم ولا كيف فالكلام والخصومة والجدال والمراء محدث يقدح الشك في القلب وإن أصاب صاحبه الحق والسنة

"Know – and may Allah have mercy on you – that there is not *qiyas* [s: rational opinion] in the *Sunnah* nor striking similitude's nor following one's desires; rather one must have full conviction in the reports and traditions of the Messenger of Allah (saw) without asking 'how', without explaining them away nor to ask 'why' or to engage in discussing and arguing about them; these are all innovations that produce doubt in the heart..."

Para.10:

ولا يقول في صفات الرب تعالى لم إلا شاك في الله تبارك وتعالى والقرآن كلام الله وتنزيله ونوره وليس مخلوقا لأن القرآن من الله وما كان من الله فليس بمخلوق وهكذا قال مالك بن أنس وأحمد بن حنبل والفقهاء قبلهما وبعدهما والمراء فيه كفر

"[...] and the Qur'an is the revealed speech of Allah which is His Light and is not created because the Qur'an is from Allah and whatever is from Allah cannot be created. This is what Malik and Ahmad Ibn Hanbal as well as all the jurists before and after them said. And to dispute in this matter is disbelief (*kufr*)..."

Para.50:

واعلم أنها لم تكن زندقة ولا كفر ولا شكوك ولا بدعة ولا ضلالة ولا حيرة في الدين إلا من الكلام وأهل الكلام والجدل والمراء والخصومة والعجب

"Know that there was no cause of heresy, disbelief, doubt, unwarranted religious innovation, misguidance and confusion in the religion except through *kalam*, is proponents and those who desire to argue, dispute quarrel and have self-conceit..."

Para. 83:

وإياك والنظر في الكلام والجلوس إلى أصحاب الكلام وعليك بالآثار وأهل الآثار وإياهم فاسأل ومعهم فاجلس ومنهم فاقتبس

"Beware of *kalam* and sitting with the proponents of *kalam*. You must stick to the traditions as well as the people of the traditions. Ask questions only to them; sit only on their gatherings and make reference only to them..."

Para.112:

وإذا أردت الإستقامة على الحق وطريق أهل السنة قبلك فاحذر الكلام وأصحاب الكلام والمراء والجدال والقياس والمناظرة في الدين فإن استماعك منهم وإن لم تقبل منهم يقدح الشك في القلب وكفى به قبولا فتهلك وما كانت قط زندقة ولا بدعة ولا هوى ولا ضلالة إلا من الكلام والجدال والمراء والقياس وهي أبواب البدع والشكوك والزندقة

"If you desire to be firm on the religion and to be on the path of the people of *Sunnah* before you, be warned against *kalam*, argumentation, disputation, quarrelling, personal opinion and debating in the religion. Listening to the people who engage in these practices even if you do not accept what they say will generate doubt in your heart and accepting it is enough to destroy you. There has never been any heresy, unwarranted religious innovation, slavery to the passions and misguidance except through *kalam*, argumentation, disputation and rational opinion. They are the doors to unwarranted religious innovation, doubt and heresy..."

Notes: on this view:

1. *Kalam* is strictly prohibited as a discipline.
2. *Kalam* and associations with it like argumentation and quarrelling are blameworthy and must be avoided.
3. *Kalam* is the root cause of heresy, doubt and misguidance.
4. The norm is submission to the traditions.
5. The normative position is following the people of traditions.
6. There is no personal or rational opinion in matters of text/traditions.

7. Disputing over whether the Qur'an is created or not is disbelief.

"A Defence of Engaging in *Kalam*: Abu 'l-Hasan al-Ash'ari's *Responsa*"

Course Module: 'Early Islamic Controversies'.
Topic: *apologetic for kalam*.
Instructor: S. Z. Chowdhury
Venue: ad-Duha Institute, London.

———◆———

- Below is an excerpt from al-Ash'ari, *Kitab al-Haththt 'ala 'l-Bahth* (= *Istihsan al-Khawd fi 'Ilm al-Kalam*) reproduced from al-Ansari al-Naysaburi's *Ghunya fi'l-Kalam*; § - *wujub al-nazar*; MSS: III Ahmet no.1916 foll. $9r^0$-$11r^0$; Landberg no.1030 (= Ahlwardt no.2112), $4v^o$-$6v^o$ and Feyzullah no. 2161/2, foll. $49v^0$-$52r^0$ printed in R. M. Frank's "Al-Ash'ari's *Kitab al-Haththt 'ala 'l-Bahth*" in *MIDEO* 18, Cairo, 1988, pp.83-152.[2]

- The text is a polemical piece against one of the foremost Hanbalite doctors of theology in his time and firebrand conservative al-Barbahari (d.329/941) vindicating at least four matters for which al-Ash'ari felt he was attacked and accused of both heresy and abandoning the way of Ahmad Ibn Hanbal (d.241/855):

[1] the permissibility of rational theology;

[2] the permissibility of *kalam* methods;

[3] the Qur'anic support for subject matters debated in *kalam*;

[4] the Prophet's engagement in subject matters debated in *kalam*.

Contention:

- The main thrust of anti-*kalam* Hanbalite theologians can be summarised into the following syllogism:

---

[2] See also *The Theology of al-Ash'ari: The Arabic Texts of al-Ash'arl's Kitab al-Luma' and Risalat Istihsan al-Khawd fi 'Ilm al-Kalam*, ed. and tr. by R. J. McCarthy (Beirut: Imprimerie Catholique, 1953) and *Risalat Istihsan al-Khawd fi 'Ilm al-Kalam* (Beirut: Dar al-Mashari', 1995).

[P1] If *kalam* was an authentic practice, then the Prophet would have practiced it;

[P2] The Prophet did not practice *Kalam*;

_____

[C] Therefore, *kalam* is not an authentic practice.

- al-Ash'ari then seeks to demonstrate the falsity of this argument with a number of responses with intellectual and textual evidences. Only response 1 and 3 will be highlighted below (where response 2 is the most extended):

Response 1: The Prophet never censured anyone who engaged in *kalam*:

قال الشيخ أبو الحسن رضي الله عنه : الجواب عنه من ثلاثة أوجهٍ : (أحدها) قلب السؤال عليهم بأن يقال : النبيُّ صلى الله عليه وآله وسلم لم يقل أيضاً إنه من بَحَثَ عن ذلك وتكلَّم فيه فاجعلوه مبتدعاً ضالاً، فقد لزمكم أن تكونوا مبتدعة ضُلّالاً إذ قد تكلمتم في شيء لم يتكلم فيه النبيُّ صلى الله عليه وآله وسلم، وضللتُم من لم يُضَلِّلهُ النبيُّ صلى الله عليه وآله وسلم .

<u>Translation</u>:

"The first response is to turn the question on the questioner: The Prophet also did not censure or label a person who studies or discusses [s: matters pertaining to *kalam*] as being a heretical innovator or misguided. You would be required to label yourselves as heretical innovators and misguided persons because you are engaged in discussing matters the Prophet (saw) never discussed. You have labelled misguided someone whom the Prophet never labelled as misguided..."

Response 3: Early figures engaged in something the Prophet did not do; are they heretics?

ثم يقال : النبيُّ صلى الله عليه وءاله وسلم لم يصحَّ عنه حديثٌ في أن القرءانَ غيرُ مخلوقٍ أو هو مخلوقٌ، فلِمَ قلتم : إنه غيرُ مخلوقٍ ؟

فإن قالوا : قد قالَه بعضُ الصحابةِ وبعضُ التابعينَ، قيلَ لهم : يلزَمُ الصحابي والتابعي مثلُ ما يلزَمُكم من أن يكونَ مبتدعًا ضَالاً إذ قالَ ما لم يقُلهُ الرسولُ صلى الله عليه وءاله وسلم .

Translation:

"It will be said to them that the Prophet (saw) did not authenticate any statement on whether the Qur'an is created or uncreated; so then why do you [emphatically] say it is uncreated? If they reply by saying: some of the Prophet's companions and their followers have stated this then it will be said to them: you will be necessitated to say of the companions and their followers what you are necessitated to say of yourselves namely that this would be tantamount to religious innovation (*bid'ah*) and misguidance (*dalalah*) because they would discussed something the Messenger (saw) did not ever discuss..."

فإن قالوا : لأنَّ أحمدَ بنَ حَنبلٍ رضي الله عنه قال بنفي خلقِهِ وتكفيرِ من قال بخلقِهِ، قيل لهم : ولِمَ لَمْ يَسكُت أحمدُ عن ذلك بل تكلَّم فيه ؟

فإن قالوا : لأن العباس العنبري ووكيعاً وعبدَ الرحمنِ بنَ مَهدِي وفلاناً وفلاناً قالوا إنه غيرُ مخلوقٍ، ومَن قال بأنَهُ مخلوقٌ فهو كافرٌ.

قيل لهم : ولِمَ لَمْ يسكُت أولئك عما سكتَ عنه صلى الله عليه وءاله وسلم فإن قالوا : لأن عمرو بن دينارٍ وسفيانَ بنَ عُيَيْنَة وجعفرَ بنَ محمدٍ رضي الله عنهم وفلاناً وفلاناً قالوا : ليسَ بخالقٍ ولا مخلوقٍ.

قيلَ لهم : ولِمَ لم يسكت أولئكَ عن هذه المقالةِ، ولم يَقُلها رسولُ الله صلى الله عليه وءاله وسلم ؟

فإن أحالوا ذلك على الصحابةِ أو جماعةٍ منهم كان ذلك مكابرةً، فإنه يقالُ لهم : فلِمَ لَم يسكتوا عن ذلك، ولم يتكلم فيه النبيُ صلى الله عليه وءاله وسلم، ولا قال : كفِّروا قائلَه، وإن قالوا : لا بدَّ للعلماءِ من الكلامِ في الحادثَةِ ليَعلَمَ الجاهلُ حكمَها، قيلَ لهم : هذا الذي أردناهُ منكُم، فلِمَ مَنَعتُم الكلامَ، فأنتم إن شئتم تكلَّمتُم حتى إذا انقطعتم قلتم : نُهينا عن الكلامِ، وإن شئتم قلَّدتُم من كان قبلَكُم بلا حُجَّةٍ ولا بيانٍ، وهذه شهوةٌ وتَحكُّمٌ.

Translation:

"If they say that [s: we discuss matters of whether the Qur'an is created or not] because Ahmad Ibn Hanbal argued for [the Qur'an's] uncreated nature and declared disbelief on the one who believes it is created, then we will respond by saying: Why did Ahmad not remain silent on this matter instead of discussing it? If they then reply by saying that because al-'Abbas al-'Anbari, al-Waki', 'Abd al-Rahman Ibn Mahdi all stated that the Qur'an was uncreated and that whoever held it to be crated was a disbeliever. We will then respond again by asking why did these figures not remain silent on a matter over which the Prophet was silent? If it said that the issue was discussed because 'Amr Ibn Dinar, Sufyan Ibn 'Uyaynah and Ja'far Ibn Muhammad all discussed it saying [the Qur'an] was neither a creator nor something created then we will ask yet again as to why they did not remain silent on a matter which the Prophet was silent about [...] if they reply and say that it is necessary for the *'Ulama'* of *kalam* in the present time to teach the ignorant the judgments regarding it then we will respond by saying: this is exactly what we wanted to hear from you. So then why do you prohibit *kalam*? [...]"

Scholastic Hanbalites 1:
The Statement of al-Mar'i Ibn Yusuf al-Hanbali –
On the Temporal nature of the World

The Temporality of the world:

وأعلم أن العالم كله محدث وقد أجمع أهل الحق على حدوثه إذ هو متغير حادث وقد ثبت بالدلائل القطعيه امتناع القول بوجود حوادث لا أول لها ففي البخاري عن عمران بن حصين قال إني عند رسول الله صلى الله عليه وسلم إذ جاءه قوم من بني تميم فسألوه عن أول هذا الأمر ماكان قال: كان الله ولم يكن شيء قبله وكان عرشه على الماء ثم خلق السموات والأرض وكتب في الذكر كل شيء...

Translation:

"Know that the entire world is temporal (*muhdath*). It has been agreed by the scholars of truth on its temporality because it is temporal and changing by definitive evidences which prevent the statement of there being temporal things that have no beginning. In the *hadith* from al-Bukhari of 'Imran Ibn Husayn who said that: Indeed I was with the Messenger of Allah (saw) when a group of people from Banu Tamim came and asked him regarding what thing was first in existence. The prophet replied: **'There was Allah and nothing with Him'**..."[3]

Notes:

- Temporal entities are contingent, i.e. they emerged in time; they are created in space and time.
- The world is a temporal entity because it undergoes change (*taghayyur*) in time.
- Temporal entities do not regress infinitely into the pass. There was a distant pass when it did not exist.
- Narration: 'Allah was and there was nothing with Him': there were no prior entities co-existing with Allah.

Also:

- Hanabalites engaged in *kalam* using both reason and revelation to give a defence of doctrine.
- The Hanbalites also had a scholastic tradition and were considered orthodox figures.

---

[3] See al-Mar'i, *Buhjat al-Nazirin wa Ayat al-Mustadallin*.

Scholastic Hanbalites 2:
The Statement of Ahmad Ibn Hanbal –
On the Negation of Allah as a Body

The rejection of Allah as 'Jism' (a body):

وأنكر أحمد على من يقول بالجسم وقال إن الأسماء مأخوذة من الشريعة واللغة، وأهل اللغة وضعوا هذا الاسم على ذي طولٍ وعرضٍ وسمكٍ وتركيبٍ وصورةٍ وتأليف والله تعالى خارج عن ذلك كله، فلم يجز أن يسمى جسمًا لخروجه عن معنى الجسمية، ولم يجيء في الشريعة ذلك فبطل

Translation:

"Ahmad [Ibn Hanbal] rejected anyone ascribing the word 'body' (*jism*) [s: to Allah]. [He said]: The Names [of Allah] are taken from the Shari'ah and the Arabic language. The people of language have designated this term [s: *jism*] to entail having length, width, thickness, parts, form or composition. Allah is excluded [s: above] all that. Thus it would not be permitted to call [Allah] a body because of Him being beyond the meanings of this description. The Shari'ah has not come with this meaning [s: to be applied to Allah] and hence it is rejected..."[4]

Notes:

- Ahmad ibn Hanbal rejects the ascription of the term *jism* to Allah.
- Ahmad denies any measurable limit or determination of Allah.
- Neither the intellect nor the Shari'ah accepts *jism* as a description for Allah.
- Ahmad engaged in polemical scholastics (*kalam*).

---

[4] Transmitted from Abu Fadl al-Tamimi the chief Hanbalite in Baghdad in *I'tiqad al-Imam Ahmad*, p.45.

Part Two: *Created Qur'an*

1) Presuppositions of the Controversy.
2) Key words in the Controversy.
3) Different Views on Qur'an being created.
4) A Summary of both Scripturalist and Rationalist Views.
5) Two early Creeds.

"Presuppositions Related to the Controversy over the Created Qur'an"

Course Module: 'Early Islamic Controversies'.
Topic: *presuppositions*.
Instructor: S. Z. Chowdhury
Venue: ad-Duha Institute, London.

───────♦───────

Mu'tazilites	Ash'arites / Maturidites	Scripturalists
1. Reason is necessary and the departure point for understanding metaphysics.	1. Reason is necessary and a departure point for understanding metaphysics.	1. Primacy of scripture over reason.
2. Scholastic lexicon as the framework within which to understand the *nature* of the Qur'an and Divine attributes.	2. Scriptural attestations must be also upheld and not denied.	2. Veneration of the Qur'anic *ipissimia verba*.
3. No compromising the absolute transcendence and uniqueness of Allah.	3. Scholastic lexicon as a useful framework within which to understand the *nature* of the Qur'an and Divine attributes.	3. The Qur'an is a mysterious embodiment of the sacred that is inexplicable.
4. Denial of any anthropomorphism or resemblance to creation.	4. No compromising the absolute power and uniqueness of Allah.	4. The early righteous generation (*salaf*) and their methodology in understanding the Qur'an is normative.
	5. Denial of any anthropomorphism or resemblance to creation.	5. Rejection of the scholastic lexicon as the framework within which to understand the *nature* of the Qur'an and Divine attributes.

A Basic Lexicon of the Qur'an Controversy

	Arabic	English
1.	*hikayah*	حكاية / 'imitation', 'transmission'.
2.	*Lawh*	لوح / 'tablet', 'record'.
3.	*huruf*	حروف / 'letters', 'symbols'...
4.	*Mithl*	مثل / 'likeness', 'resemblance'.
5.	*Sawt*	صوت / 'voice', 'sound'.
6.	*Mahall*	محل / 'loci', 'place', 'abode'.
7.	*Makhluq*	مخلوق / 'created'.
8.	*Ma'ani*	معاني / 'meanings', 'forms', 'significations'.
9.	*kalimah*	كلمة / 'word', 'utterance'.
10.	*Rasm*	رسم / 'impression', 'form', 'sketch', 'written'.
11.	*'ibarat*	عبارة / 'expressions', 'articulations', 'wording'.
12.	*Maqru'*	مقروء / 'that which is recited', 'the eternal speech of Allah'.
13.	*lafz*	لفظ / 'word', 'utterance'.
14.	*dalalat*	دلالة / 'Indications of the Divine Word', 'ramifications'.
15.	*Kalam*	كلام / 'speech', 'logos'
16.	*Mushaf*	مصحف / 'codex', 'volume', 'bound book of the Qur'an'.
17.	*Muhdath*	محدث / 'originated', 'temporal', 'created', 'emergent'.
18.	*Sifah*	صفة / 'attribute', 'quality', 'property'.
19.	*Azali*	أزلي / 'pre-eternal'.
20.	*Nafsi*	نفسي / 'pertaining to the Essence of Allah'.

"Letters, Sounds and Speech:
Surveying Early Views on the Qur'an's Creation"

Course Module: 'Early Islamic Controversies'.
Topic: *survey of views*.
Instructor: S. Z. Chowdhury
Venue: ad-Duha Institute, London.

———◆———

Background:

- *Khalq al-qur'an*: = the doctrine of the created nature of the Qur'an.
- Deep scholastic divisions amongst early Muslims over this controversy.
- The controversy became a dividing line between orthodoxy and heresy.
- Some questions that were asked include:

1. How does divine eternal speech manifest in the temporal realm without restricting divine attributes of Power?

2. How to explain Qur'anic assertions of divine speech (*kalam*) without compromising transcendence?

3. How to strike a balance between the excessive veneration of the *ipissima verba* and its co-eternality with Allah.

- The controversy is still kept alive today in polemical discussions and exchanges between Muslims.

- Below is a basic survey of views recorded by al-Ash'ari in his *Maqalat al-Islamiyyin* – a book on early Muslim heresiology:

[1] Survey:

§1. The Iraqi Precursors:
Basic Mu'tazilite 'Substrate-Instantiationism'

Text: al-Ash'ari's *Maqalat al-Islamiyyin*, pp.118-120.

والفرقة الثالثة من المعتزلة يزعمون ان القرآن مخلوق لله وهو عرض وابوا ان يكون جسما وزعموا انه يوجد في اماكن كثيرة في وقت واحد اذا تلاه تال فهو يوجد مع تلاوته وكذلك اذا كتبه كاتب وجد مع كتابته وكذلك اذا حفظه حافظ وجد مع حفظه فهو يوجد في الاماكن بالتلاوة والحفظ والكتابة ولا يجوز عليه الانتقال والزوال وهذا قول ابى الهذيل واصحابه وكذلك قوله في كلام الخلق انه جائز وجوده في اماكن كثيرة في وقت واحد

والفرقة الرابعة منهم يزعمون ان كلام الله عرض وانه مخلوق واحالوا أن يوجد في مكانين في وقت واحد وزعموا ان المكان الذي خلقه الله فيه محال انتقاله وزواله منه ووجوده في غيره وهذا قول جعفر بن حرب واكثر البغداذيين

والفرقة الخامسة منهم اصحاب معمر يزعمون ان القرآن عرض والاعراض عندهم قسمان قسم منها يفعله الاحياء وقسم منها يفعله الاموات محال ان يكون ما يفعله الاموات فعلا للاحياء والقرآن مفعول وهو عرض ومحال ان يكون الله فعله في الحقيقة لأنهم يحيلون ان تكون الاعراض فعلا لله وزعموا ان القرآن فعل للمكان الذى يسمع منه ان سمع من شجرة فهو فعل لها وحيثما سمع فهو فعل للمحل الذى حل فيه

والفرقة السادسة يزعمون ان كلام الله عرض مخلوق وانه يوجد في اماكن كثيرة في وقت واحد وهذا قول الاسكافى

واختلفت المعتزلة في كلام الله هل يبقى ام لا يبقى فمنهم من قال هو جسم باق والاجسام يجوز عليها البقاء وكلام المخلوقين لا يبقى وقالت طائفة اخرى كلام الله تعالى عرض وهو باق وكلام غيره يبقى وقالت طائفة اخرى كلام الله عرض غير باق وكلام غيره لا يبقى وقالت في كلامه تعالى انه لا يبقى وانه انما يوجد في وقت ما خلقه الله ثم عدم بعد ذلك

واختلفت المعتزلة هل مع قراءة القارىء لكلام غيره وكلام نفسه كلام غيرهما على مقالتين فزعمت فرقة منهم ان مع قراءة القارىء لكلام غيره وكلام نفسه كلاما غيرهما وزعمت فرقة اخرى منهم ان القراءة فى الكلام

واختلف الذين زعموا ان مع القراءة كلاما على مقالتين فزعمت الفرقة الاولى منهم ان القراءة كلام لأن القارىء يلحن في قراءته وليس يجوز اللحن الا في كلام وهو ايضا متكلم وان قرأ كلام غيره ومحال ان يكون متكلما بكلام غيره فلا بد من ان تكون قراءته هي كلامه وقالت الفرقة الثانية القراءة صوت والكلام حروف والصوت غير الحروف

واختلفت المعتزلة في الكلام هل هو حروف ام لا على مقالتين فزعمت فرقة منهم ان كلام الله سبحانه حروف وزعم آخرون منهم ان كلام الله سبحانه ليس بحروف

واختلفت المعتزلة في الكلام هل هو موجود مع كتابته ام لا على مقالتين فزعمت فرقة منهم ان الكلام يوجد مع كتابته في مكانها كما يجامع القراءة في موضعها وزعمت فرقة اخرى منهم ان الكتابة رسوم تدل عليه وليس بموجود معها

View 1: - Abu 'l-Hudhayl: The Qur'an is created and is an *'arad* ('accident') but not a *jism* ('body'/'tangible entity'); it exists in many places simultaneously, e.g. 1) it exists wherever

41

and whenever its recitation is; 2) wherever and whenever it is written down and 3) wherever and whenever it is memorised; it can neither perish not become extinct from its original etching on the Divine Tablet (*lawh*) by Allah which is essentially its substrate. || **Abu 'l-Hudhayl: The Qur'an was created as an *'arad* on the Preserved Tablet (*lawh*) ⟶ then it was revealed to the temporal realm ⟶ this temporal realm instantiates the Qur'an or invokes its existence and non-existence depending on whether it is writing, reading or memorising.**

View 2: - Mu'ammar: There is no uncreated Divine speech or Word that corresponds to a divine attribute in Allah; Allah only creates bodies and not accidents so He did not create a pre-existent Qur'an on the Preserved Tablet as an accident (*'arad*); there is No Eternal and Archetypal Word/Speech of Allah but *mediated* instantiations by bodies/entities like bushes, Angels, Prophets, etc that have been created with a capacity by Allah to convey what He communicates. The Qur'an therefore is an instantiation from a capacity to create or act (*fi'l*) from the *loci* (*mahall*) it is heard, e.g. the burning bush is the *loci* from which the Qur'an is heard and hence an act of the bush. The Qur'an then is a fully temporal origination from temporal entities || Mu'ammar: **Allah communicates to objects and entities ⟶ these objects and entities have a capacity given by Allah to instantiate the Qur'an from their own acts ⟶ what we hear therefore of the Qur'an is a production from the capacity of objects and so there is no Original Qur'an or Divine Speech.**

View 3: - Ja'far Ibn Harb as well as the Baghdadi Mu'tazilites: held that the Qur'an was created and impossible for the same Qur'an to be in two places at once; they argued that the Qur'an was created to inhere in a location (*mahall*; ['encompassed surrounding', 'substrate']) from which it can be transferred, perish, exist or come into being. || **Ja'far Ibn Harb: Divine speech = created in a location ⟶ the Qur'an in this location can now undergo changes whether that means being instantiated or not-instantiated.**

View 4: Whether the speech of Allah is the letters of a language or not (where '=' is that of *identity*).

View 5: Whether the speech of Allah subsists or not where some argued it did because it is a *jism* and they have the property to subsist whereas others argued it cannot because it is an *'arad* and they do not subsist.

View 6: Whether the recitation is tantamount to speech because one can commit mistakes in recitation which is only possible if they were words/speech. Whether recitation is the actual speech of the person reciting or the speech of another is disputed. To be considered a 'speaker' (*mutakallim*) is to speak one's own words and the words of another.

View 7: Whether the speech of Allah is existent in the place that it is being written down.

View 8: Whether the speech of Allah is merely indicated by or expressed by letters but not existent when it is being written down.

§2. The People of Hadith (*ashab al-hadith*)

Text: al-Ash'ari's *Maqalat al-Islamiyyin*, p.171.

ويقولون ان القرآن كلام الله غير مخلوق والكلام في الوقف واللفظ من قال باللفظ او بالوقف فهو مبتدع عندهم لا يقال اللفظ بالقرآن مخلوق ولا يقال غير مخلوق

View: The Qur'an is Allah's divine and uncreated speech and its words are neither said to be created nor uncreated. One cannot reserve judgement either on the issue as that is tantamount to heresy (= Qur'anic *modalism*).

§3. Early Murji'a Positions

Text: al-Ash'ari's *Maqalat al-Islamiyyin*, p.98.

واختلفت المرجئة في القرآن هل هو مخلوق ام لا على ثلاث مقالات فقال قائلون منهم انه مخلوق وقال قائلون منهم انه غير مخلوق وقال قائلون منهم بالوقف وانا نقول كلام الله سبحانه لا نقول انه مخلوق ولا غير مخلوق

View 1: The Qur'an is created.

View 2: The Qur'an is not created.

View 3: Non-Committal – neither created not uncreated.

§4. Early Shi'ite Views

Text: al-Ash'ari's *Maqalat al-Islamiyyin*, p.32.

واختلف الروافض في القرآن وهم فرقتان : الفرقة الاولى منهم هشام بن الحكم واصحابه يزعمون ان القرآن لا خالق ولا مخلوق وزاد بعض من يخبر على المقالات في الحكاية عن هسام فزعم انه كان يقول لا خالق ولا مخلوق ولا يقال ايضا غير مخلوق لانه صفة والصفة لا توصف وحكى «زرقان» عن هشام بن الحكم انه قال القرآن على ضربين ان كنت تريد المسموع فقد خلق الله عز وجل الصوت المقطع وهو رسم القرآن فأما القرآن فهو فعل الله مثل العلم والحركة لا هو ولاهو غيره. والفرقة الثانية منهم يزعمون انه مخلوق محدث لم يكن ثم كان كما تزعم المعتزلة والخوارج وهؤلاء قوم من المتأخرين منهم

View 1: Hisham ibn al-Hakam – the Qur'an is an attribute of Allah and hence cannot be created; it is not a creator and neither is it created. A reported opinion of Hisham from Zurqan is that the Qur'an's form is the voice or that which is heard in recitation is incarnate in the human voice or sound but the Qur'an itself is an act of Allah (*fi'l Allah*) like His knowledge or movement but not Allah Himself nor other than Himself.

View 2: The Qur'an is created and is temporal (*muhdath*) and did not exist at a prior time t_0 but then came into being at a point in time t_1 as held by the Mu'tazila, Khawarij and later adherents of these sects.

Specific references: H. Wolfson, *The Philosophy of the Kalam*, pp.112-132, 147-197; L. Gardet and A. Grohman, art. "Kalam" in *Encyclopaedia of The Holy Qur'an*, ed. by Agwan et al, pp.675-680; J. Bowker, *Picturing God*, pp.123-128; W. M. Watt, *Formative Period of Islamic Thought*, pp.279-297 and F. E. Peters, *A Reader on Classical Islam*, pp.172-173).

[2] Ibn Kullab:

§5. Enter 'Ma'na': Ibn Kullab's Opaque Entity

Text: al-Ash'ari's *Maqalat al-Islamiyyin*, pp.315-316.

قال عبد الله بن كلاب ان الله سبحانه لم يزل متكلما وان كلام الله سبحانه صفة له قائمة به وانه قديم بكلامه وان كلامه قائم به كما ان العلم قائم به والقدرة قائمة به وهو قديم يعلمه وقدرته وان الكلام ليس بحروف ولا صوت ولا ينقسم ولا يتجزأ ولا يتبعض ولا يتغاير وانه معنى واحد بالله عز وجل وان الرسم هو الحروف المتغايرة وهو قراءة القرآن وانه خطأ ان يقال كلام الله هو هو او بعضه او غيره وان العبارات عن كلام الله سبحانه تختلف وتتغاير وكلام الله سبحانه ليس بمختلف ولا متغاير كما ان ذكرنا لله عز وجل يختلف ويتغاير والمذكور لا يختلف

ولا يتغاير وانما سمى كلام الله سبحانه عربيا لأن الرسم الذى هو العبارة عنه وهو قراءته عربى فسمى عربيا لعلة وكذلك سمى عبرانيا لعلة وهى ان الرسم الذى هو عبارة عنه عبرانى...

وزعم عبد الله بن كلاب ان ما نسمع التالين يتلونه هو عبارة عن كلام الله عز وجل وان موسى عليه السلام سمع كلام الله متكلما بكلامه وان معنى قوله فاجره حتى يسمع كلام الله معناه حتى يفهم كلام الله

View: Allah has the attribute (*sifa*) of speech (*kalam*) ‖ It is eternal with Him and eternally part of Him just like His attributes of knowledge and power. His Divine speech is not 1) in the actual form or appearance of letters; 2) it is not manifested through voice; 3) it is not divisible; 4) it is not composite; 5) it is not atomic (*yataba''ad*); 6) it is unchanging; 7) it is a singular 'form'/'signification'/'meaning' (*ma'na wahid*) ‖ The appearance (*rasm*) are the changing letters which the Qur'an's recitation is composed of and it is fallacious to either fully or partially equate this with Allah's eternal and divine speech or to negate it of Him. The recitation (*qira'a*) is not the Word/Speech of Allah but what is recited (*al-makru'*) is. ‖ The manner of expression (*'ibarat*) of Allah's speech varies and changes but the divine and eternal attribute of speech does not change ‖ Arabic or Hebrew is merely the linguistic modality or vehicle through which the divine speech is expressed or manifest. Therefore, the recitation of the Qur'an that one hears is a mode of expression of Divine speech and not the actual word of Allah and so when Musa heard Allah speak (Q. 9:6), the reference is actually to his *comprehension* and *understanding* of what was spoken. ‖ **Ibn Kullab: Divine speech = *ma'na* ⟶ the Qur'an = a representation of this *ma'na* through language ⟶ this representation is temporal and thus mediated through Angel Gabriel to the Prophet Muhammad.**

General references: H. Daiber, *Das Theologische-Philosophische System des Mu'ammar*, pp.169-172; J. Van Ess, "Ibn Kullab un die Mihna", pp.98-137; H. Wolfson, *The Philosophy of the Kalam*, pp.248-250; R. Fernhout et al, *Canonical Text Bearers of Absolute Authority*, pp.124-145; J. Peters, *God's Created Speech*, pp.1-6; R. Wisnovsky, *Avicenna's Metaphysics in Context*, pp.234-237 and B. Jokisch, *Islamic Imperial Law: Harun al-Rashid's Codification Project*, pp.358-364.

"Battle for 'The Word': Summarising Rationalists and Scripturalist Views:"

Course: 'Early Islamic Controversies'
Topic: *Comparison of views*
Instructor: S. Z. Chowdhury
Venue: Ad-Duha Institute, London

Below is a table of the divergence between rationalists and scripturalists regarding the ontological status of the Qur'an:

Rationalists

8th / 1st - 2nd century – Jahm Ibn Safwan: The Qur'an is something 'created' (*makhluq*) based on several arguments:

(1)

[P1] Everything other than Allah is created;
[P2] The Qur'an is other than Allah,
Therefore,
_____

[C1] The Qur'an is something created.

(2)

[P3] All attributes must inhere in a body (*jism*);
[P4] 'Speaking' is an attribute,
Therefore,
_____

[C2] Speaking must inhere in a body
But Allah is not a body and so Allah does not have the attribute of speaking.

8th – 9th / 2nd – 3rd Century – the Mu'tazilites:

Scripturalists

٢٨٨ - سألت أبي رحمه الله عن قوم يقولون : لما كلم الله عز وجل موسى لم يتكلم بصوت فقال أبي : بلى إن ربك عز وجل تكلم بصوت ، هذه الأحاديث نرويها كما جاءت .

وقال أبي رحمه الله : حديث ابن مسعود رضي الله عنه : إذا تكلم الله عز وجل سمع له صوت كجر السلسلة على الصفوان⁽¹⁾ قال أبي وهذا الجهمية تنكره⁽²⁾ .

٢٨٩ - وساق أبو يعلى - بسنده - عن أبي بكر الخلال حدثنا محمد ابن علي قال : حدثنا يعقوب بن بختان قال : سئل أبو عبد الله عمن زعم أن الله لم يتكلم بصوت . قال : بلى يتكلم سبحانه بصوت⁽³⁾ .

٢٩٠ - وأخرجها الخلال من طريق آخر عن يعقوب بزيادة : وهذه الأحاديث نرويها لكل حديث وجه يريدون على الناس من زعم أن الله لم يكلم موسى فهو كافر⁽⁴⁾ .

٢٩١ - وأخرج أبو بكر الخلال عن المروذي قال : سمعت أبا عبد الله وقيل له إن عبد الوهاب⁽⁵⁾ قد تكلم وقال : من زعم أن الله كلم موسى بلا صوت فهو جهمي عدو لله عدو للإسلام . فتبسم أبو عبد الله وقال : ما أحسن ما قال ، عافاه الله⁽¹⁾ .

٢٩٢ - قال أبو يعلى : وقد نص أحمد في رواية الجماعة على إثبات الصوت⁽²⁾ .

(*al-Masa'il*, 1:302-303 #288-292)

Ahmad Ibn Hanbal: "[Allah] spoke with a voice" (#288); "Allah's voice is heard like chains that drag on the rock" (#289).

Allah really speaks and possesses the attributes of

46

Allah is described validly as a *mutakallim* ('speaker') *but not on account of Himself* but on account of another, i.e. by creating the property of speaking in a person or thing. This is because only 'bodies' (*ajsam*) have properties/accidents and so Allah cannot carry properties/accidents. Therefore He does not speak Himself and does not actually have the attribute of 'speaking'.

3rd – 4th / 9th – 10th century – Ibn Kullab, al-Ash'ari and al-Maturidi:

> Allah 'speaks' and has this eternal attribute without any location, restriction, letters, sounds, voice, etc. because these are *contingent properties of things* and will subject Him to change and occurrences. Therefore, Allah has His own internal 'form' (*ma'na*) of speaking (= ⟶ *kalam nafsi*).

⟶

> The Qur'an that is recited, read and written is an expression, quotation, representation or 'facsimile' of the eternal *form/word* in Allah Himself.

speaking and does so through letters and voices and sounds *but unlike any creaturely letter, voice or sound*. With regards to the Qur'an, there are few aspects:

1. The reciter (*qari*).
2. The act of recitation (*tilawah*).
3. The recited data (*maqru'*).
4. The pronounced contents (*malfuz*); ⟶ 3 & 4 are eternal and uncreated.

باب

ذكر اللفظية والتحذير من رأيهم ومقالاتهم

واعلموا رحمكم الله أن صنفاً من الجهمية اعتقدوا بمكر قلوبهم وخبث آرائهم وقبيح أهوائهم أن القرآن مخلوق، فكنوا عن ذلك ببدعة اخترعوها تمويهاً ويهرجة على العامة؛ ليخفى كفرهم، ويستغمض إلحادهم على من قل علمه وضعفت نحيزته، فقالوا: «إن القرآن الذي تكلم الله به وقاله؛ فهو كلام الله غير مخلوق، وهذا الذي نتلوه ونقرؤه بألسنتنا ونكتبه في مصاحفنا ليس هو القرآن الذي هو / كلام الله، هذا حكاية لذلك، فما نقرؤه نحن حكاية لذلك القرآن بألفاظنا نحن، وألفاظنا به مخلوقة؛ فدققوا في كفرهم، واحتالوا لإدخال الكفر على العامة بأغمض مسلك، وأدق مذهب، وأخفى وجه؛ فلم يخف ذلك بحمد الله ومنه وحسن توفيقه على جهابذة العلماء والنقاد العقلاء حتى بهرجوا ما دلسوا وكشفوا القناع عن قبيح ما ستروه؛ فظهر للخاصة والعامة كفرهم وإلحادهم، وكان الذي فطن لذلك وعرف موضع القبيح منه الشيخ الصالح، والإمام العالم العاقل أبو عبد الله ـ أحمد بن محمد بن حنبل ـ رحمه الله ـ، وكان بيان كفرهم بيناً واضحاً في كتاب الله عز وجل وسنة نبيه محمد ﷺ.

(Ibn Batta, *Ibanat al-Kubra*, 1:317-318)

The belief that the Qur'an that we have at present is an 'expression' (*hikayah*) of Allah's words is heretical.

Summary:

- The scripturalists argue that Allah speaks and the understanding must be literal.

- The rationalists argue that a literal acceptance of Allah speaking implies being bound by sounds, letters and a voice which further implies changes in Allah and this is impossible.

- These views have created the early divergence that has continued to divide Muslim views up until the present time.

An Early Scripturalist Creed:
The 'Creed' of Ibn Khuzaymah (d. 311/923)

———•———

The Arabic text from al-Dhahabi's *Siyar al-A'lam al-Nubala'*, vol.14, p.381 from the biographical segment on Ibn Khuzayma outlining what is a entirely scripturalist position on Divine Speech and how it is to be understood:

القرآن كلام الله تعالى وصفة من صفات ذاته ليس شيء من كلامه مخلوق ولا مفعول ولا محدث فمن زعم أن شيئا منه مخلوق أو محدث أو زعم أن الكلام من صفة الفعل فهو جهمي ضال مبتدع وأقول لم يزل الله متكلما والكلام له صفة ذات ومن زعم أن الله لم يتكلم إلا مرة ولم يتكلم إلا ما تكلم به ثم انقضى كلامه كفر بالله وأنه ينزل تعالى إلى سماء الدنيا فيقول هل من داع فأجيبه فمن زعم أن علمه تنزل أوامره ضل ويكلم عباده بلا كيف استوى على العرش لا كما قالت الجهمية إنه على الملك احتوى ولا استولى وإن الله يخاطب عباده عودا وبدءا ويعيد عليهم قصصه وأمره ونهيه ومن زعم غير ذلك فهو ضال مبتدع

Translation:

"The Qur'an is the speech (*kalam*) of Allah the Most High and is one of the attribute from amongst the attributes of His Essence. Nothing from His Speech is neither created (*makhluq*), nor (*maf'ul*) and nor temporal (*muhdath*). Whoever alleges that anything from [s: His Speech] is either created or temporal or alleges that speech is one of His attributes of action (*sifat al-fi'l*), then he is a misguided Jahmite innovator. And I say: Allah has never ceased to be a *mutakallim* (one who speaks) and Speech is an attribute of His essence. And whoever alleges that Allah spoke once and did not speak except what He already spoke with [s: that one time] and then His speech expired, his statement amounts to disbelief in Allah. And whoever alleges that [Allah] descends to the lowest heaven where He says, **'Is there any supplicant to whom I respond'** and additionally alleges that it is His knowledge and command that descends, then he has gone astray. And He will speak to His servants without how (*bi-la kayf*). And {**The Most Merciful ascended over the Throne**}, not in the manner held by the Jahmites that He has encompassed the dominion and not that 'he conquered it' (*istawla*). Allah Indeed speaks to His servants repeatedly and recurrently and repeats to them His narrations (*qisas*), His commands and His prohibitions and anyone who claims otherwise is a straying innovator (*dal mubtadi'*)..."

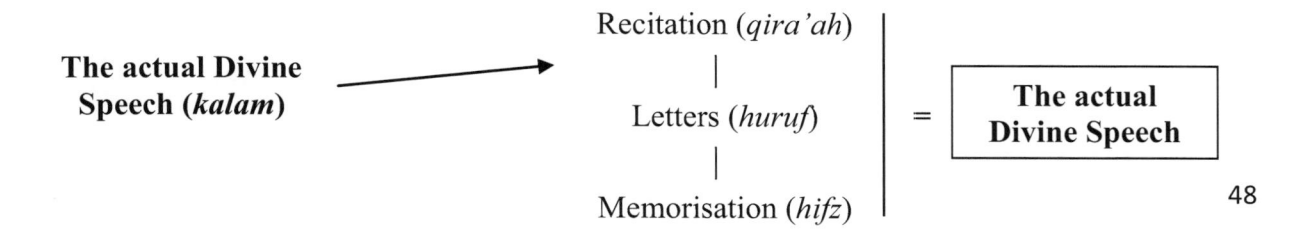

The actual Divine Speech (*kalam*) → Recitation (*qira'ah*) | Letters (*huruf*) | Memorisation (*hifz*) = **The actual Divine Speech**

An Early Ash'arite Text:
The 'Creed' of Abu Ishaq al-Isfara'ini (d. 418/1027).

The Arabic text from Abu 'l-Qasim al-Ansari's *Sharh al-Irshad*, fol.21b (= reproduced in al-Qurtubi's *al-Jami' li-Ahkam al-Qur'an*) from R. Frank's edited edition, MS Hasan Hüsnü Paşa no.1160/5, Fr. 51 in "Al-Ustadh Abu Ishak: An *Akida* together with selected Fragments", *MIDEO* 19, Louvain, 1989, pp.156 and 190-191. This is a rationalist position on how to understand the Divine Speech and its relation to temporal entities:

قال الأستاذ أبو إسحاق: اتفق أهل الحق على أن الله تعالى خلق في موسى عليه السلام معنى من المعاني أدرك به كلامه كان اختصاصه في سماعه، وأنه قادر على مثله في جميع خلقه واختلفوا في نبينا عليه السلام هل سمع ليلة الإسراء كلام الله، وهل سمع جبريل كلامه على قولين؛ وطريق أحدهما النقل المقطوع به وذلك مفقود، واتفقوا على أن سماع الخلق له عند قراءة القرآن على معنى أنهم سمعوا العبارة التي عرفوا بها معناه دون سماعه له في عينه

Translation:

"The master Abu Ishaq [al-Isfara'ini] said: the people of Truth are in agreement that Allah Most High created in Musa (peace be upon him) a type of *ma'na* (s: 'attribution', 'form', 'signification') with which he comprehended His [Divine] Speech. The specification was in his listening to it. And they are in agreement that He is able to do this in any of His creation. There is disagreement over our Prophet (upon him be peace) and whether he heard the Speech of Allah on the night of al-Isra' or whether Jibril caused him to hear it. There are two opinions here: one of the ways [s: to understand it] is to accept the transmitted evidence on this but this is not entirely satisfactory. There is agreement over the creation hearing when the Qur'an is being recited but in the meaning that they hear an articulation or expression (*'ibarah*) through which its meaning is comprehended without actually listening to it actually and directly..."

Divine Speech *(kalam)* → | **Prophet Musa's comprehension is a specific *capacity* or *power* created in him by Allah to comprehend the speech.**

↓

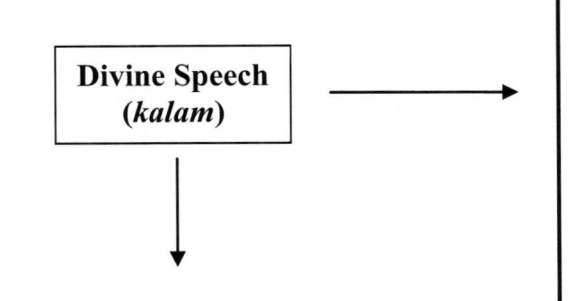

The Divine Speech is *mediated*, or *expressed*, *articulated* through letters, words and sounds (= **language**) - - - - - - → This is what humans hear in Qur'anic recitation, i.e. the expressed and instantiated speech of the Divine and it is this that is directly heard and understood and not the actual eternal speech within the Divine person.

Part Three: *Divine Attributes*

1) The Controversy: Theological Backdrop.
2) Understanding the problem of divine attributes: Ibn al-Jawzi.
3) Understanding the Arabic Language.
4) *Ta'wil*.
5) Examples of *Ta'wil* by Early Muslims.
6) A Unified Creed: al-Ash'ari.

"The Controversies Begin Here:
The Implications of the Essence and Attributes Distinction:"

Course Module: 'Early Islamic Controversies'.
Topic: *background*
Instructor: S. Z. Chowdhury
Venue: ad-Duha Institute, London.

———◆———

Early Muslim theologians like the Mu'tazilites and the sunni-*kalam* theologians discussed the nature of God's attributes (*sifat*) and His essence (*dhat*) and their relation giving rise to perplexing paradoxes. Much of this was adapted and appropriated form concepts in antiquity (e.g. sameness/otherness, identity/difference, unity/multiplicity...). The context in Islamic speculative discussions was upholding the Divine unity (*tawhid*) and transcendence (*tanzih*). The implications were wide-reaching impacting three major areas of inquiry:

[1] The Nature of Allah	[2] The Qur'an	[3] Hermeneutics
How are we to understand the Divine? Is He a set of abstract properties or a personal Creator?	What is the nature of the Qur'an? What is its status (ontological question)? How do we know what it communicates (epistemological question)?	How are we to understand scriptural references to the Creator? Can we ever know everything the Qur'an communicates about Allah?

Mu'tazilite speculation:

Linguistic studies and semantics informed Muslim debates about divine attributes and their relation to the divine essence. Mu'tazilite presuppositions about Allah were:

1. Absolute unity (no multiplicity in the divinity).
2. Absolute transcendence (no co-existence with anything in creation).

What negates 1 & 2 above are:

1. Anthropomorphism.
2. Polytheism.
3. Corporealism.

The Mu'tazilites held an equivalence between the terms *ism* ('name'), *sifah* ('attribute') and *wasf* ('description'). Thus, for them, anyone discussing divine attributes was in fact discussing about the divinity. For example, if one were to accept physical descriptions about Allah in the Qur'an as they came whether it mentions an attribute or a name of Allah, then this would entail direct affirmation of the ontological reality of these attributes; but this would undermine Divine transcendence and so must be rejected. A typical Mu'tazilite arguments would be:

[P1] If the essence of Allah and His attributes are identical, then scriptural references to Divine attributes are not real;

- (because: Allah just is the totality of His attributes),
- (because: an *ism*, *sifah* and *wasf* are identical in what they mean and stand for),
- (because: the divinity cannot instantiate contraries, e.g. 'to possess something identical to and not identical to His Essence');
- (because: a description of something physical is to directly describe its nature as physical).

[P2] The essence of Allah and His attributes are identical;

[C1] *Therefore*, scriptural references to Divine attributes are not real.

This kind of reasoning was seen by Mu'tazilite thinkers as the rational manoeuvre to make in order to negate theological paradoxes such as:

'A Plural of Eternalities'	By rejecting Allah had 'life' (*hayat*), 'power' (*qudrah*), 'will' (*iradah*) and 'knowledge' (*'ilm*) – this was reported to have been done by Wasil Ibn 'Ata' (d. 748).
'Multiplicity'	By denying divine self-descriptions – this was reported to have been done by Abu'l-Hudhayl al-'Allaf (d. 841).
'Anthropomorphism'	By rejecting scriptural references to divine physical properties as metaphorical and not real.

Problems:

Reducing the divine attributes to the essence strips Allah of his personal character which a believer uses to build h/her relationship with the Creator and so disconcertingly resembles the outlook of earlier pagan Greeks than the personal Creator of the Qur'an. Also, by over-emphasising transcendence, the Divine aspect of imminence is eliminated and perhaps this is why mysticism and Mu'tazilism rarely merged. Moreover, upholding absolute transcendence and drawing an equivalence between divine attributes and essence, paradoxically undermines revelation itself in that scriptural references to intimacy (Q. 2:187), beneficence (52:28) and forgiveness (4:106) would have no real meaning, significance and content.

References: R. M. Frank, *Beings and their Attributes*, pp.1-92 and N. El-Bizri, "God: Essence and Attributes", in *The Cambridge Companion to Classical Islamic Theology*, pp.121-124.

"Understanding the Contention: Ibn al-Jawzi's Convenient Outline"

Course Module: 'Early Islamic Controversies'.
Topic: *the contentions*
Instructor: S. Z. Chowdhury
Venue: ad-Duha Institute, London.

———◆———

There are a number of contentions that have led early scholars to hold utterly divergent views with regard to understanding scriptural references to Allah. Ibn al-Jawzi (d.597/1201) conveniently outlines the points of contention in his treatise *Daf' Shubh al-Tashbih* were he absolves the eponym of his school Ahmad Ibn Hanbal (d.242/855) from any association with a form of textual literalism that certain senior Iraqi Hanbalite scholars were propounding in his name. He lists seven errors his colleagues fell into ranging from theological assumptions to methodological problems.

Below is the text from the original Arabic (= M. Z. al-Kawthari edn, pp.27-31; H. Saqqaf edn, pp.104-107 and English trans. in A. H. Ali, *The Attributes of God*, pp.57-50 and M. Swartz, *A Medieval Critique of Anthropomorphism*, pp.125-129):

فصل قلت: وقد وقع غلط المصنفين الذين ذكرتهم في سبعة أوجه: أحدها: أنهم سموا الأخبار أخبار صفات، وإنما هي إضافات، وليس كل مضاف صفة، فإنه قال سبحانه وتعالى: ونفخت فيه من روحي الحجر: .وليس لله صفة تسمى روحا، فقد ابتدع من سمى المضاف صفة . الثاني: أنهم قالوا: إن هذه الأحاديث من المتشابه الذي لا يعلمه إلا الله تعالى. ثم قالوا: نحملها على ظواهرها، فواعجبا!! ما لا يعلمه إلا الله أي ظاهر له..؟! فهل ظاهر الاستواء إلا القعود، وظاهر النزول إلا الانتقال ..الثالث: أنهم أثبتوا لله تعالى صفات، وصفات الحق لا تثبت إلا بما يثبت به الذات من الأدلة القطعية .الرابع: أنهم لم يفرقوا في الأحاديث بين خبر مشهور كقوله: " ينزل إلى السماء الدنيا " وبين حديث لا يصح كقوله: " رأيت ربي في أحسن صورة " بل أثبتوا بهذا صفة وبهذا صفة الخامس: أنهم لم يفرقوا بين حديث مرفوع إلى النبي – صلى الله عليه وسلم – وبين حديث موقوف على صحابي أو تابعي، فأثبتوا بهذا ما أثبتوا بهذا .السادس: أنهم تأولوا بعض الألفاظ في موضع ولم يتأولوها في موضع آخر كقوله: " من أتاني يمشي أتيته هرولة ." قالوا: هذا ضرب مثل للإنعام .وروي عن عمر بن عبد العزيز أنه قال: " إذا كان يوم القيامة جاء الله يمشي " فقالوا: نحمله على ظاهره . السابع: أنهم حملوا الأحاديث على مقتضى الحس فقالوا: ينزل بذاته وينتقل ويتحرك، ثم قالوا: لا كما يعقل. فغالطوا من يسمع فكابروا الحس والعقل فحملوا الأحاديث على الحسيات...

[1] The Hanbalite literalists assumed that every grammatical possessive construct (*idafah* = 'the X belongs to/is possessed of some Y') related to Allah stood for an *attribute* of Allah, e.g. when Allah states 'My soul', it does not follow that Allah has an attribute called 'a soul' but this is what appeared to be there assumption.

[2] The Hanbalite literalists argued that texts with ambiguous (*mutashabih*) meanings are unknown although they are taken literally (*'ala zahirihi*). This is contradictory as declaring the meaning to be unknown but stating it as literal *is* to designate a modality of meaning to it, e.g. the meaning of word *W* is known only to Allah but *W* is taken literally is self-contradictory.

[3] Attributes described of Allah can only be established through definitive proofs (*adillah qat'iyyah*) and not narrations with solitary transmission channels (*ahad*) or those indicating less than definitive levels.

[4] The Hanbalite literalists established attributes of Allah through well-known traditions as well as inauthentic traditions without careful scrutiny or discrimination. This is of course flawed and dangerous.

[5] The Hanbalite literalists failed to differentiate between a report established from the Prophet himself (*marfu'*) and a report from a Companion of the Prophet (*mawquf*). The latter cannot be an absolute authority in creed that is binding on Muslims as only the Prophet can establish matters of theology.

[6] The Hanbalite literalists are arbitrary in their interpretations of textual reports. Sometimes they commit to *ta'wil* whereas at other times they insist on the literal meaning, e.g. 'running' is figuratively interpreted as Divine 'benevolence' (*al-in'am*).

[7] The Hanbalite literalists interpret the textual references to qualities and attributes according to human perception, e.g. 'descending', 'moves from place to place' and 'shifting' This generates confusion in the listener and brings impressions of actual movement in the mind especially with the additional qualification 'in Himself' or 'in His Essence' (*bi-dhatihi*) which appears not to be supported by any textual proof.

"Understanding The Arabic Language:
Some Outlines"

Course Module: 'Early Islamic Controversies'.
Topic: *the Arabic Language*
Instructor: S. Z. Chowdhury
Venue: ad-Duha Institute, London.

- It is imperative to understand the Arabic language because it is the language of revelation (*wahy*).[5]

- Misunderstanding and weakness in the Arabic language will be detrimental to correct belief, jurisprudence and exegetical endeavours of the Qur'an and *hadith*.[6]

- Before even unpacking some of the thorny issues related to the Divine descriptions in the Qur'an and *hadith* literature, it is highly important to be familiar with the sources and categories of significations and designations afforded to Arabic words within the Arabic language.[7]

- Unless we know how Arabs understood their language, we cannot begin to understand the Qur'an.[8]

ARABIC WORDS AND THEIR DESIGNATIONS
= 4 general types

[1] *Haqiqi* (= literal, real, lexical, original meaning).	[2] *Majazi* (= non-literal, figurative, metaphorical meaning).	[3] *ishtiqaq* (= derived words from a consonantal root, i.e. the basic verb).	[4] *ta'rib* (= arabising a word, i.e. making it Arabic and part of the language).

---

[5] 'Ata' ibn Khalil, *al-Taysir ila Usul al-Tafsir* (Beirut: Dar al-Ummah, 1998; 2nd edn. 2006), pp.20-22.
[6] Ibid, pp.22-23.
[7] Ibid, pp.17-20.
[8] Ibid, p.17f.

Meaning:

- **The *haqiqi* meaning**: This has three sub-categories:[9]

[1a] *al-haqiqah al-lughawiyyah* (the lexical or linguistic meaning):

= the original meaning designated by the Arabs for that word, e.g. *ra's*/رأس which means the uppermost part of a body, i.e. the 'head'.

Sometimes this is also referred to as the 'lexical sense', 'apparent meaning' or 'surface meaning'.

[1b] *al-haqiqah al-'urfiyyah* (the customary meaning):

= the meaning of a word that the Arabs have come to now use that substitutes the original lexical meaning, e.g. *dabbah*/دابة which originally means 'everything that crawls on the earth' but is used by the Arabs to mean 'every four-legged creature'.

Part of this type is the 'specific customary usage of words' (*al-haqiqah al-'urfiyyah al-khassah*) and these words include technical vocabulary within each discipline or specialised area of study, e.g. the word *fa'il*/فاعل generally means 'someone who does an act' but in Arabic grammar it means the grammatical 'subject'.[10]

[1c] *al-haqiqah al-shar'iyyah* (the legal meaning):

= the meaning given to a word defined by Allah and His Messenger, e.g. the word *salah*/صلاة linguistically means *du'a'* ('supplication') but it technically means specific actions that involve bowing and prostrating (i.e. 'prayer') as defined in the manuals of *fiqh*.

- **The *majazi* meaning**: this has many types such as:[11]

[2a] *Majaz mursal* ('metonymy'): this is where a *haqiqi*

[2b] *Majaz 'aqli* ('the rational metaphorical

[2c] *al-Isti'arah* ('the metaphor'): this is where there is a

[2d] *al-Kinayah* ('the rhetorical allusion'): this is a comparison

---

[9] Ibid, p.16.
[10] Ibid, p.16.
[11] Ibid, pp.16-17. Cf. the outlines and discussion on *haqiqah-majaz* division given by Sh. Taqi al-Din al-Nabhani in *al-Shakhsiyyah al-Islamiyyah* (2nd edn al-Quds: n.p. 1953), vol.3, pp.131-136.

meaning of a word cannot be taken at all.	expression'): this is where something is attributed to a person or thing that is not literally compatible to him.	comparison between two things or ideas that cannot be literally taken.	of sorts between one thing and another with the possibility of it being read and taken in its literal meaning.
Example: Q. 2:19 {...**they put their fingers in their ears**} meaning they put their 'finger tips' into their ear-holes as it is impossible for it to mean inserting the entire finger.[12]	**Example**: 'The king built the city',[13] i.e. he never actually built anything but rather it was the workers and builders; what is meant is that the king made the city famous, successful and famed.	**Example**: 'I climbed up to the *ra's* of the mountain', i.e. 'I climbed up to the **top** of the mountain'. The word *ra's* means the head IR uppermost part of an animal or person and here metaphorically refers to the mountain top because a mountain literally does not have a head.	**Example**: 'The one who sleeps until the morning' (*na'um al-duha*/نؤوم الضحى) referring to the pampered girl in her house.[14] Here there is no *qarinah* ('contextual indication') preventing the literal meaning to be taken as this expression could refer to a girl who does actually sleep until late in the day.

---

[12] Imam al-Shawkani comments in *Fath al-Qadir* (Beirut: Dar al-Fikr, n.d.), vol.1, p.48:

وقوله: { يَجْعَلُونَ أَصْبِعَهُمْ فِى ءاذَانِهِم } جملة مستأنفة لا محل لها كأنّ قائلاً قال: فكيف حالهم عند ذلك الرعد؟ فقيل: يجعلون أصابعهم في آذانهم. وإطلاق الإصبع على بعضها مجاز مشهور، والعلاقة الجزئية والكلية لأن الذي يجعل في الأذن إنما هو رأس الإصبع لا كلها...

"And Allah saying {**they put their fingers in their ears**} is a new sentence [...] mentioning the entire finger is a really a reference to part of it and this metaphor is well known. The relationship is between the part and the whole because what is inserted into the ear is the tip of the finger, not all of it..."

[13] Arabic: *bana'l-amir al-madinah* / بنى الأمير المدينة || An example in English would be 'the football manager built that club', i.e. he did not actually build anything; what is meant is that he made the club famous, successful and famed.

[14] 'Ata' ibn Khalil, *al-Taysir ila Usul al-Tafsir*, pp.18-19. Another example in English would be the expression, 'she's such a princess', meaning she needs pampering and is spoilt as a person. However, it is quite possible that the expression actually refers to girl who really is a princess, i.e. of royal descent and hence can be carried on a literal reading.

- Thus *majaz* refers to a departure from the *haqiqi* meaning of a word to a non-literal meaning of that word as used by Arabs within their language **based on an indication that requires it**.[15]

Morphology:

- **[3] The *ishtiqaq* designation**: this is where a word is derived from its consonantal root in a form that fits the pattern of the Arabic nouns even if that form may not have actually been used by the Arabs, e.g. the consonantal root *s / l / m* [س / ل / م] has its derived forms, *salam*/سلام, *salim*/سليم, *salim*/سالم, *silm*/سلم and many more and so if the form *salman*/سلمان were to be used, it would be a valid word pattern as it fits the stencil *fa'lan*/فعلان even though the Arabs have not actually used this and it would still be considered a sound Arabic word. The rule is that as long as a word is derived from its tri-consonantal root and fits a valid Arabic word-pattern.[16]

- **[4] The *ta'rib* designation**: the Arabs have over time (even before the advent of Islam) made words that became part of their language, i.e. they *arabised* the word and incorporated it into their lexical stock. By 'arabised' is meant giving the word a valid Arabic noun pattern (*wuzn*). For example, the word *istabraq*/إستبرق ('fine silks') is of Persian origin but entered into the classical language (and hence the Qur'an; see Q. 55:54) in the form of *istaf'al*/إستفعل.[17]

- Therefore, there are 4 types of designation for the Arabic word (*kalimah/lafz*). Words must fall into one of these types otherwise it will not be considered correct according to Arabic usage, i.e. how the Arabs understood and employed their own language:

Meaning:

- Literal or *haqiqi*: 1. *lughawiyyah*; 2. *'urfiyyah* and 3. *Shar'iyyah*.

- Non-literal or *majazi*: 1. *majaz mursal*; 2. *majaz 'aqli*; 3. *isti'arah* and 4. *kinayah*.

---

[15] al-Nabhani, *al-Shakhsiyyah al-Islamiyyah*, vol.3, p.131.
[16] 'Ata' ibn Khalil, *al-Taysir ila Usul al-Tafsir*, pp.17-18.
[17] See A. Jeffery, s.v. "istabraq" in *The Foreign Vocabulary of the Qur'an* (Leiden: E. J. Brill, 1938 repr. 2007), pp.58-60.

Morphology:

- Derived or *ishtiqaq*.
- Arabised or *ta'rib*.

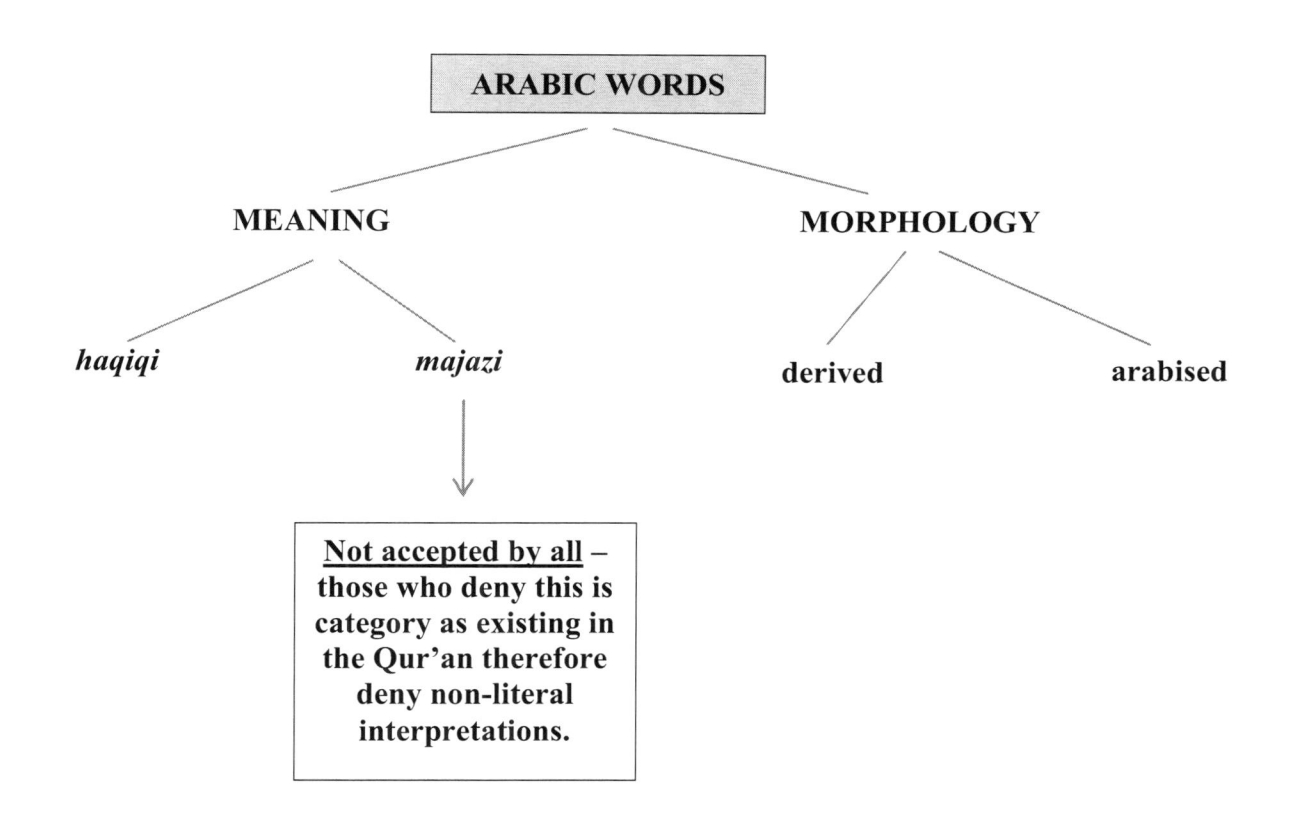

```
                    ARABIC WORDS
                   /            \
              MEANING          MORPHOLOGY
              /     \           /       \
          haqiqi  majazi    derived   arabised
                     |
                     v
```

Not accepted by all – those who deny this is category as existing in the Qur'an therefore deny non-literal interpretations.

"TA'WIL"

Course: 'Early Islamic Controversies'
Topic: *ta'wil*
Instructor: S. Z. Chowdhury
Venue: Ad-Duha Institute, London

———◆———

A number of matters will be outlined regarding this topic:

1. What are the *mutashabihat* of the Qur'an?
2. What is the need for the *mutashabihat* contents?
3. What is *ta'wil*?
4. Implications on theology and approaching and understanding the Qur'an.

Key verse under discussion: Chapter Al 'Imran Verse number 7.

هُوَ ٱلَّذِىٓ أَنزَلَ عَلَيْكَ ٱلْكِتَٰبَ مِنْهُ ءَايَٰتٌ مُّحْكَمَٰتٌ هُنَّ أُمُّ ٱلْكِتَٰبِ وَأُخَرُ مُتَشَٰبِهَٰتٌ ۖ فَأَمَّا ٱلَّذِينَ فِى قُلُوبِهِمْ زَيْغٌ فَيَتَّبِعُونَ مَا تَشَٰبَهَ مِنْهُ ٱبْتِغَآءَ ٱلْفِتْنَةِ وَٱبْتِغَآءَ تَأْوِيلِهِۦ ۗ وَمَا يَعْلَمُ تَأْوِيلَهُۥٓ إِلَّا ٱللَّهُ ۗ وَٱلرَّٰسِخُونَ فِى ٱلْعِلْمِ يَقُولُونَ ءَامَنَّا بِهِۦ كُلٌّ مِّنْ عِندِ رَبِّنَا ۗ وَمَا يَذَّكَّرُ إِلَّآ أُو۟لُوا۟ ٱلْأَلْبَٰبِ ۝٧

{It is He who has sent down to you, [O Muhammad], the Book; in it are verses [that are] *muhkamat* - they are the foundation of the Book - and others that are *mutashabihat*. As for those in whose hearts is deviation [from truth], they will follow that of it which is unspecific, seeking discord and seeking a *ta'wil* [suitable to them]. And no one knows its [true] *ta'wil* except Allah and those who are firmly rooted in knowledge who say, 'We believe in it. All [of it] is from our Lord.' And no one will be reminded except those of understanding}.

[1] The *Mutashabih*:

- The Qur'anic verses are of two types: *muhkam* and *mutashabih*. This is mentioned in Q. 3:7. It is the latter category that has been given extended treatment by scholars because of the implications it holds for theology and Linguistic beauty of the Qur'an.

وفي المتشابه سبعة أقوال. أحدها: أنه المنسوخ، قاله ابن مسعود، وابن عباس، وقتادة، والسدي في آخرين. والثاني: أنه ما لم يكن للعلماء إلى معرفته سبيل، كقيام الساعة، روي عن جابر بن عبد الله. والثالث: أنه **الحروف المقطعة** كقوله: «**ألم**» ونحو ذلك، قاله ابن عباس. والرابع: أنه ما اشتبهت معانيه، قاله مجاهد. والخامس: أنه ما تكررت ألفاظه، قاله ابن زيد. والسادس: أنه ما احتمل من التأويل وجوهاً. وقال ابن الأنباري: المحكم ما لا يحتمل التأويلات، ولا يخفى على مميّز، والمتشابه: الذي تعتوره تأويلات. والسابع: أنه القصص، والأمثال، ذكره القاضي أبو يعلى

"There are seven opinion regarding the *mutshabihat*: the first is it refers to the abrogated contents of the Qur'an according to Ibn Mas'ud, Ibn 'Abbas, Qatadah and al-Suddi; the second is that it is that which the scholars have no way of knowing like the when the end of time will occur and this was related from Jabir Ibn 'Abd Allah; the third is that it refers to the dislocated letters like <<**Alif – Lam - Mim**>> and those like it. This is what Ibn 'Abbas held; the fourth is where the meanings are not clear as mentioned by Mujahid; the fifth is that it refers to those words repeatedly occurring. This was the opinion of Ibn Zayd; the sixth is that it refers to that which carries many interpretations. Ibn al-Anbari said: the *muhkam* is something that does not admit of different interpretations and whose meaning is not obscure whereas the *mutashabih* is that which is exposed to many interpretations; the seventh is that it refers to narratives and parables. This was mentioned by al-Qadi Abu Ya'la…"

- The differences between the *muhkam* and *mutashabih* are given below in the table:

Muhkam	Mutashabih
1. That which abrogates.	1. That which is abrogated.
2. The *halal* and the *haram*.	2. That which cannot be known.
3. The interpretation of which is known.	3. It is the dislocated letters.
4. That which is not abrogated.	4. That which has ambiguous meanings.
5. Those words not constantly repeated.	5. Those words that repeatedly occur.
6. That which requires no additional	6. That which admits many meanings.

clarification.

7. That which only carries one interpretation.	7. Parables and narratives.

- Ibn al-Jawzi then explains the reason for there being *mutashabihat* in the Qur'an:

فإن قيل: فما فائدة إنزال المتشابه، والمراد بالقرآن البيان والهدى؟ فعنه أربعة أجوبة. أحدها: أنه لما كان كلام العرب على ضربين. أحدهما: الموجز الذي لا يخفى على سامعه، ولا يحتمل غير ظاهره. والثاني: المجاز، والكنايات، والإشارات، والتلويحات، وهذا الضرب الثاني هو المستحلى عند العرب، والبديع في كلامهم، أنزل الله تعالى القرآن على هذين الضربين، ليتحقق عجزهم عن الإتيان بمثله، فكأنه قال: عارضوه بأي الضربين شئتم، ولو نزل كله محكماً واضحاً، لقالوا: هلا نزل بالضرب المستحسن عندنا. ومتى وقع في الكلام إشارة أو كناية، أو تعريض أو تشبيه، كان أفصح وأغرب.

"If it is asked what is the point in revealing *mutashabih* verses when the purpose of the Qur'an is a divine clarification and guidance? This has four responses: One of the responses is because the speech of the Arabs is of two types: one is the speech that is not ambiguous to the one who hears it and so cannot be other than the apparent [lexical] sense and the second is figurative such as metonymy, allusions and intimations and this second type is the most beautiful according to the Arabs and most embellished when it comes to their speech. Allah thus revealed the Qur'an according to these two types in order to show their inability to produce something like it as if to say, 'produce something like it from either of the types you want'. If the Qur'an was only revealed with *muhkam* and clear verses then they would have asked, 'if only it was revealed in the most excellent form of our language'. Thus, whenever linguistic features such as allusions, metonymy, similes and periphrasis occur, it makes the speech eloquent and exhortative…"

[2] The *Ta'wil*:

- Linguistically, the word "ta'wil" from the root *a / w / l /* which linguistically means to return to the origin; in the Qur'an, it has come with the meanings of: 1) *tafsir*; explanation, exegesis, interpretation; 2) *'aqibah*; the awaited outcome of some matter; 3) *yawm al-qiyamah*; the Day of Judgment and 4) *ru'yah*; dreams or visions.

- Below is a table of the basic differences between *ta'wil* and *tafsir*:

Tafsir	*Ta'wil*
علم يعرف به فهم كتاب الله المنزل على نبيه وبيان معانيه،	الفقه هو فهم المعنى المراد

واستخراج حكمه وأحكامه (al-Zarkashi, *al-Burhan*, 1:13)	والتأويل ادراك االحقيقة التى يؤول اليها المعنى (Ibn al-Qayyim, *I'lam*, 1:332)
1. Explanation based on early reports.	1. Explanation based on personal understanding.
2. Explanation based on authoritative transmission (*riwayah*).	2. Explanation based on reports understanding and research (*dirayah*).
3. Explanation based on semantic and linguistic analysis.	3. Explanation based on application of a verse.
4. Explanation based on the literal sense.	4. Explanation based on non-literal/allegorical/figurative sense.

- Ibn Kathir states:

كما تقدم عن ابن عباس رضي الله عنهما أنه قال: التفسير على أربعة أنحاء: فتفسير لا يعذر أحد في فهمه، وتفسير تعرفه العرب من لغاتها، وتفسير يعلمه الراسخون في العلم، وتفسير لا يعلمه إلا الله، ويروى هذا القول عن عائشة وعروة وأبي الشعثاء وأبي نَهِيك وغيرهم.

"As was mentioned earlier where Ibn 'Abbas (Allah be pleased with them both) said: explanations are of four types: [1] an explanation that no-one has an excuse not to know; [2] explanation that the Arabs know from their dialects; [3] an explanation of those endowed with intelligence and [4] explanation that none but Allah knows…"

---

[1] Refers to necessary matters related to the religion such as the meanings of "tawhid", the Day of Judgment, "iman", "salah", "taharah", etc.

[2] Refers to the specific language of the Arabs and their ordinary lexical stock;

[3] Refers to the specialised knowledge that those with deep and rooted knowledge alone possess;

[4] Refers to the matters that are comprehended but their realities not fully known, e.g. "Paradise", "Hell", "the Day of Judgement", etc.

[3] Theological Implications:

1. The *mutashabih* can be known by the specialists.
2. The *mutashabih* data have a sense (*madlul*) but it is ambiguous.
3. There is no stigma attached to the *mutashabih* data.
4. Part of the Arabic language is its *mutashabih* category which enriches it and beautifies it.
5. If the *mutashabih* is taken to mean the ambiguous contents, then that opens up possibilities for *ta'wil*.
6. Rationalists accept *ta'wil* as a possibility and sometimes even consider it necessary.

References: Ibn al-Jawzi's *Zad al-Masir*, s.v. Q.3:7; Ibn Kathir, *Tafsir al-Qur'an al-'Azim*, 2:8-11, s.v. Q. 37 – cf. M. Ayoub, *The Qur'an and its Interpreters: Vol 2*, pp.20-46 as well as A. Rippin, "Tafsir" in M. Eliade (ed.) *The Encyclopaedia of Religion*, pp.236-241 and I. Poonawala, "Ta'wil" in *EI²*, 10:390-392.

"An Inventory of Divine Attributes and their Interpretation"

Course: 'Early Islamic Controversies'
Topic: *list of divine attributes*
Instructor: S. Z. Chowdhury
Venue: Ad-Duha Institute, London

    Below is a table with a catalogue of scripturalist and rationalist interpretations of creaturely ascriptions of Allah found in the Prophetic literature taken from Ibn al-Jawzi's *Daf' Shubh al-Tashbih* ('Dispelling the Doubts of Anthropomorphism').

Cover of the Manuscript of *Daf' Shubh al-Tashbih*,
MS Şehit Ali 1561

Hadith Canon	Ascription	Scripturalist Reading	Rationalist Reading
Bukhari (= *Fath al-Bari*, 11:3); Schwarz, *Medieval Critique*,	صورة ‖ Adam created in the 'form' of His Lord.	Literal expression is taken;	'Form' here is not in the sense of 'lines' (*takhatit*) but

pp.170-176, Ali, *Attributes*, pp.67-69.

Allah has a form unlike any other form;

signification (abstract/non-perceptible), e.g. Adam was created according to *Divine characteristics* for example of life, knowledge, etc. in order to distinguish him from all other creatures.

Adam was created in the form of an angel or created with an unprecedented likeness.

Hadith:

الحديث الأول روى البخاري في الصحيحين من حديث أبي هريرة رضي الله عنه قال: قال رسول الله صلى الله عليه وسلم: خلق الله آدم على صورته

"al-Bukhari mentions from the *Sahihayn* a hadith from Abu Hurayrah (Allah be pleased with him) who said that the Messenger of Allah said: **'Allah created Adam according to [H]is form'**…"

Ibn al-Jawzi remarks:

وإن الصورة ها هنا معنوية لا صورة تخاطيط، وقد ذهب أبو محمد بن قتيبة في هذا الحديث إلى مذهب قبيح فقال: لله صورة لا كالصور فخلق آدم عليها... وهذا تخليط وتهافت لأن معنى كلامه: إن صورة آدم كصورة الحق. وقال القاضي أبو يعلى: " يطلق على الحق تسمية الصورة لا كالصور كما أطلقنا اسم ذاته." قلت: وهذا تخليط، لأن الذات بمعنى الشئ، وأما الصورة فهي هيئة وتخاطيط وتأليف، وتفتقر إلى مصور ومؤلف وقول القائل لا كالصور، نقض لما قاله، وصار بمثابة من يقول: جسم لا كالأجسام، فإن الجسم ماكان مؤلفا، فإذا قال: لا كالأجسام نقض ما قال

"The meaning of 'form' here is in signification and not in the sense of lines and limits. Ibn Qutaybah interpreted this tradition of the Prophet in a very flawed way. He said: Allah has a form not like any other form and created Adam upon it. But this is confusing and incoherent because what his words actually mean is: 'Adam's form is like the Form of the One True God'. al-Qadi Abu Ya'la said: 'It is permitted to ascribe the Real with a form but not like any other form in the way He can be ascribed with a Essence'. I say: this too is a confused and muddled statement because an essence signifies the quintessence of something whereas a form of something implies a shape with limits and composition that would require a form-giver and composer. Therefore, the one who says 'a form not like any other form' contradicts himself. It is the same as saying, 'a body but not like any other body' because a body just is something composite. If it is said, 'not like any other body' it is also a contradiction…" (*Daf' Shubh al-Tashbih*, p.174 (Saqqaf's edn.) and 49-50 (Kawthari's edn). = *Kitab Akhbar al-Sifat*, p.175-176); cf. Ibn Furak's ascription of this view to Ibn Qutaybah,

Mushkil al-Hadith, p.67f; Abu Ya'la, *al-Mu'tamad*, 58 and al-Baghdadi, *Tabaqat al-Hanabilah*, 1:212.).

Ascription		Scripturalist Interpretation	Rationalist Interpretation
'jealousy'	*ghirah*	Attribute; literal	It means Allah's 'dislike'.
'foot'	*qadam*	Attribute; literal	It means those lowest and worst of Allah's creatures'; it can also mean 'group'/ 'party' as in a swarm (*qadam*) of locusts.
'laugh'	'dahk'	Attribute; literal	It means to reveal a matter – here Allah's generosity; The Arabs say the earth is said to have 'laughed' when it reveals its flowers ‖ *dahikat al-ard bi'l-nabat idha zahara ma fiha*: ضحكت الأرض بالنبات إذا ظهر ما فيها، وانفتق عن زهره، كما يقال :بكت السماء.
'wing'	'kanaf'	Attribute; literal	It means 'Mercy', 'Kindness', 'protection', screen'.
'descent'	'nuzul'	Attribute, literal	It means: Allah's mercy descends; Allah's mercy coms close.
'hand'	'yad'	Attribute, literal	It means 'hand', 'power', 'strength', 'favour', 'good treatment'.
'face'	'wajh'	Attribute, literal	It means 'essence'.
'eyes'	''uyun'	Attribute, literal	It means 'care', 'supervision',

Scripturalist reading:

All Islamic scriptural references to qualities, attributes, emotions and actions of Allah are taken on this view according to their outward or apparent meanings because of the following presuppositions:

1. Words are taken literally.

2. Taking them non-literally means to deny, negate, alter and change what Allah has described of Himself.
3. These are divine attributes.
4. This is how the descriptions and reports have been understood by early Muslims.
5. The mind cannot be used to preclude the literal/apparent meaning.
6. The formula 'x but not like any other x' applied to Allah is correct and meaningful.

Rationalist reading:

All Islamic scriptural references to qualities, attributes, emotions and actions of Allah are taken on this view according to their non-literal meanings because of the following presuppositions:

1. Words are taken literally unless there is a warrant to depart from it.
2. Taking them literally leads one to actually affirming for the divinity creaturely attributes.
3. Not every possessive construct ('belonging to…') is a divine attribute.
4. Sometimes physical descriptions about Allah are for pedagogical and instructional purposes.
5. Early Muslims have understood divine ascriptions non-literally.
6. The mind can be used to preclude the literal/apparent meaning.
7. The formula 'x but not like any other x' applied to Allah is meaningless and contradictory.

Both positions desire the same aim, the transcendence of Allah and disassociating Him from any creaturely resemblance. However, their difference is conceptual and methodological presuppositions (refer to the 'Presuppositions' section above).

"Taken other than Literally: The *Ta'wil* of Ibn Abbas"

Course: 'Early Islamic Controversies'
Topic: *ta'wil of Ibn Abbas*
Instructor: S. Z. Chowdhury
Venue: Ad-Duha Institute, London

Below are four examples of non-literal interpretations by the senior expert of Qur'anic exegesis taught by the Prophet Himself Ibn Abbas:

"saq" / ساق	"nisyan" / نسي	"nur" / نور	"kursi" / كرسي
قال جماعة من الصحابة و التابعين من أهل التأويل يبدو عن أمر شديد...	اي ففي هذا اليوم، وذلك يوم القيامة نساهم، يقول نتركهم في العذاب...	عن ابن عباس ... يقول: الله سبحانه هادي أهل السموات والأرض	عن سعيد بن جبير، عن ابن عباس: { وَسِعَ كُرْسِيُّهُ } قال: كرسيه: علمه.
(al-Tabari, *al-Jami' al-Bayan*, 29:38)	(al-Tabari, *al-Jami' al-Bayan*, 8:201)	(al-Tabari, *al-Jami' al-Bayan*, 18:135)	(al-Tabari, *al-Jami' al-Bayan*, 3:7)
"A group of the Companions and Tabi'un from the people of *ta'wil* interpreted it to mean 'a serious matter'…"	"In other words, 'on this day which is the Day of Judgment where We will forget you' [Ibn Abbas] said it means: 'we will abandon you and leave you to a severe punishment…"	"From Ibn Abbas […] who said: 'Allah – glory be to Him! – is 'the one who guides in the heavens and the earth'…"	"From Sa'id Ibn Jubayr from Ibn Abbas on: {**His *kursi* encompasses the heavens and the earth**} to mean 'His Knowledge'…"

The Source of Ibn Abbas' Exegesis

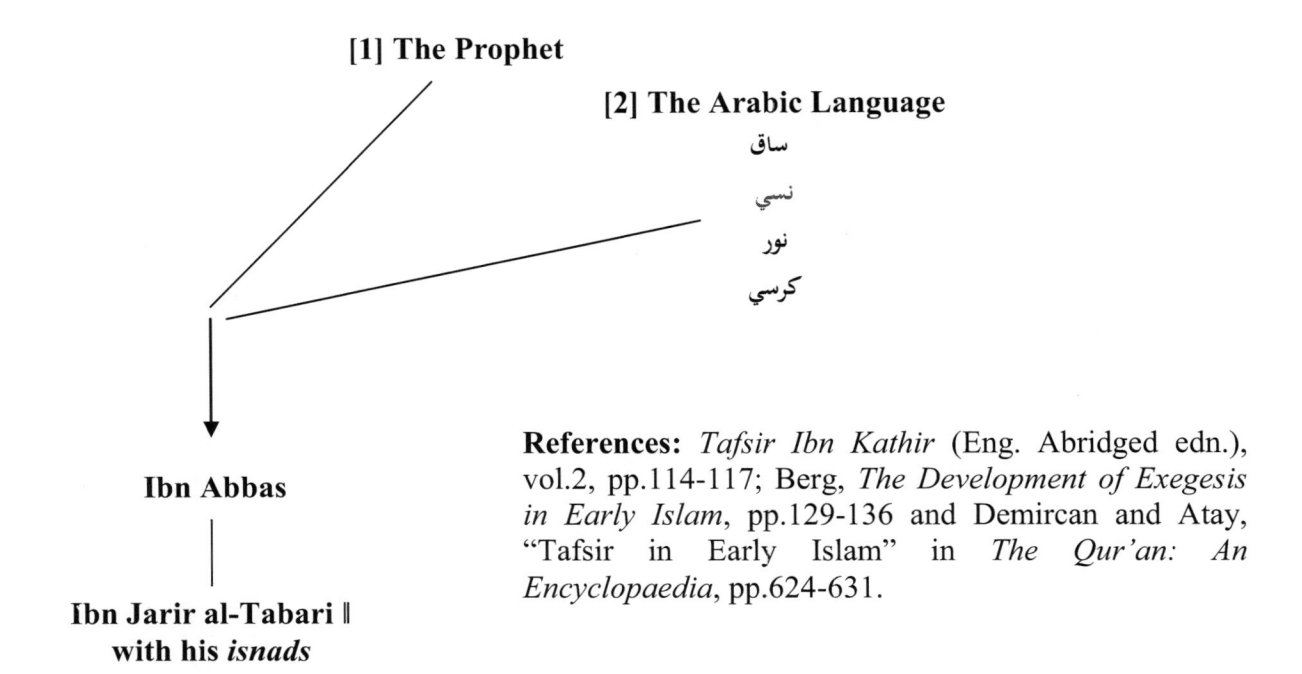

[1] The Prophet

        [2] The Arabic Language

ساق

نسي

نور

كرسي

Ibn Abbas

Ibn Jarir al-Tabari
with his *isnads*

References: *Tafsir Ibn Kathir* (Eng. Abridged edn.), vol.2, pp.114-117; Berg, *The Development of Exegesis in Early Islam*, pp.129-136 and Demircan and Atay, "Tafsir in Early Islam" in *The Qur'an: An Encyclopaedia*, pp.624-631.

"Sufyan al-Thawri Performed *Ta'wil*"

Course Module: 'Early Islamic Controversies'.
Topic: *Ta'wil of Sufyan al-Thawri*.
Instructor: S. Z. Chowdhury
Venue: ad-Duha Institute, London

———◆———

- Imam Sufyan al-Thawri makes *ta'wil* of Allah's "establishment on the Throne" (*istiwa'*):

وأوّل سفيان الثوري الاستواء على العرش: بقصد أمره، والاستواء إلى السماء: بالقصد إليها

"Sufyan al-Thawri made *ta'wil* of {*istiwa'* on the Throne} by saying it means 'a matter **concerning His command**' and {*istiwa'* towards the heavens when it was smoke} means 'he ***proceeded towards*** it'..."

Reference: See al-Juwayni, *Kitab al-Irshad*, pp.59-60 and 'Ali al-Qari, *Mirqat al-Mafatih*, 2:137.

"al-Awza'i Performed *Ta'wil*"

Course Module: 'Early Islamic Controversies'.
Topic: *Ta'wil of al-Awza'i*.
Instructor: S. Z. Chowdhury
Venue: ad-Duha Institute, London

- Imam al-Awza'i makes *ta'wil* of Qur'anic verses as mentioned by Imam al-Nawawi:

هَذَا الْحَدِيثِ مِنْ أَحَادِيثِ الصِّفَاتِ وَفِيهِ مَذْهَبَانِ مَشْهُورَانِ لِلْعُلَمَاءِ سَبَقَ إِيضَاحهمَا فِي كِتَاب الْإِيمَان وَمُخْتَصَرهمَا أَنَّ أَحَدهمَا وَهُوَ مَذْهَب جُمْهُور السَّلَف وَبَعْض الْمُتَكَلِّمِينَ : أَنَّهُ يُؤْمِن بِأَنَّهَا حَقّ عَلَى مَا يَلِيق بِاَللَّهِ تَعَالَى وَأَنَّ ظَاهِرهَا الْمُتَعَارَف فِي حَقّنَا غَيْر مُرَاد وَلَا يَتَكَلَّم فِي تَأْوِيلهَا مَعَ اِعْتِقَاد تَنْزِيه اللَّه تَعَالَى عَنْ صِفَات الْمَخْلُوق وَعَنْ الِانْتِقَال وَالْحَرَكَات وَسَائِر سِمَات الْخَلْق . وَالثَّانِي : مَذْهَب أَكْثَر الْمُتَكَلِّمِينَ وَجَمَاعَات مِنْ السَّلَف وَهُوَ مَحْكِيّ هُنَا عَنْ مَالِك وَالْأَوْزَاعِيّ : أَنَّهَا تُتَأَوَّل عَلَى مَا يَلِيق بِهَا بِحَسْب مَوَاطِنهَا....

"This kind of *hadith* is from the *hadith* of the divine attributes (*al-sifat*) and regarding it there are two well known school or positions of the scholars both discussed in the 'Book of Iman' earlier but in summary here: the first, and it is the school of the majority of the *salaf* and some of the Mutakallimun is those who believe in [s: these divine attributes] as true and real according to what befits Allah Most High, and that the *zahir* meaning that we commonly apply to ourselves is not what is meant and that one does not speak regarding its interpretation while holding the belief that Allah Most High is free from the attributes of the created, and from translocation, and movement, and the rest of the attributes of created beings. The second is the school of the majority of the Mutakallimun and a group from amongst the *Salaf* **and it is what is reported from Malik and al-Awza'i that they are interpreted figuratively (*tata'awwala*) but only according to their appropriate contextual meanings.**"

Reference: al-Nawawi, *Sharh Sahih Muslim*, 1:376.

"Malik Performed *Ta'wil*"

Course Module: 'Early Islamic Controversies'.
Topic: *Ta'wil of Malik ibn Anas*.
Instructor: S. Z. Chowdhury
Venue: ad-Duha Institute, London

———◆———

- Imam Malik's *ta'wil* of Allah's "descent" (*nuzul*):

سئل الإمام مالك – رحمه الله – عن نزول الرب عزّ وجلّ، فقال (ينزل أمره – تعالى – كل سَحَر، فأما هو عزّ وجلّ فإنه دائم لا يزول ولا ينتقل سبحانه لا إله إلى هو) اه.

"Imam Malik (Allah have mercy on him) was asked regarding the 'descent' of the Lord (Most Exalted and High) and he said: 'The **command** of your Lord – Most High – descends every night. As for if it is Allah Himself [s: who descends], then He is everlasting and does not move from one place to another may He be glorified! There is none but Him!"

Reference: See Ibn 'Abd al-Barr, *Kitab al-Tamhid*, 7:143; Ibn Kathir, *Siyar al-A'lam al-Nubala'*, 8:105 and al-Nawawi, *Sharh Sahih Muslim*, 6:37.

"Ahmad ibn Hanbal Performed *Ta'wil*"

Course Module: 'Early Islamic Controversies'.
Topic: *Ta'wil of Ahmad*.
Instructor: S. Z. Chowdhury
Venue: ad-Duha Institute, London

———◆———

- Imam Ahmad's *ta'wil* of Allah's "coming" (*maji'*):

روى البيهقي عن الحاكم عن عمرو بن السماك عن حنبل أن أحمد بن حنبل تأوّل قول الله تعالى (وجاء ربك) أنه جاء ثوابه. ثم

قال البيهقي: وهذا إسناد لا غبار عليه اه.

"al-Bayhaqi reports from al-Hakim from 'Amr b. al-Sammak from Hanbal from Ahmad b. Hanbal who made *ta'wil* of Allah's statement Most High {**And your Lord came**} as meaning 'Allah's **reward** came'..."

_____

Reference: See Ibn Kathir, al-*Bidaya wa'l-Nihaya*, 10:361.

ISTIWA':
A Term from the *Mutashabihat* Category

Course: 'Early Islamic Controversies'
Topic: *istiwa'*
Instructor: S. Z. Chowdhury
Venue: Ad-Duha Institute, London

―――――◆―――――

Allah says in the Qur'an al-Karim: {**It is He who has created for you everything that is in the earth and then turned towards the Heavens and fashioned it as seven and He has knowledge of all things** [Q. 2:29]}. Shaykh 'Ata' Ibn Khalil comments:

﴿ هُوَ ٱلَّذِى خَلَقَ لَكُم مَّا فِى ٱلۡأَرۡضِ جَمِيعًا ثُمَّ ٱسۡتَوَىٰٓ إِلَى ٱلسَّمَآءِ فَسَوَّىٰهُنَّ سَبۡعَ سَمَٰوَٰتٍۚ وَهُوَ بِكُلِّ شَىۡءٍ عَلِيمٌ ﴾

إن الله سبحانه قد خلق جميع الأشياء في الأرض لينتفع الإنسان بها، وهذا من الأدلة على أن الأصل في الأشياء الإباحة، ثم استوى سبحانه إلى السماء أي عمد لخلقها بعد الأرض دون خلقه شيئا بينهما، والعرب تقول استوى إليه أي قصده قصدا مستويا دون أن يلوي على شيء غيره قاله الفراء، وهذا ما أرجحه في معنى (استوى) هنا، وأقول أرجحه لأن (استوى) من المتشابه. وأتم سبحانه خلق السموات فجعلها سبعا والله سبحانه عليم بكل شيء من خلقه.

Sh. 'Ata' Ibn Khalil, *al-Taysir fi Usul al-Tafsir*, 67.

"Allah – Glory be to Him! – created all things in the earth so that human beings can benefit from it and this is a proof text for the rule that 'in origin, all things are permissible'. Then He – Glory be to Him! – *turned* (*thumma'stawa*) to the heavens meaning he resolved or intended to create it after creating the earth without Him creating anything else in between. When the Arabs say *istawa ilayhi*, it means 'to have an absolute resolve for something and not for anything else'; this was held by al-Farra'. This is perhaps the closest meaning to the word "*istawa*" in this context. I say 'the closest meaning' because the word "*istawa*" is from the *mutashabih* category…"

"*Istiwa'* - Revisited:
Some Early Views of Theologians"

Course: 'Early Islamic Controversies'
Topic: *istiwa' revisited*
Instructor: S. Z. Chowdhury
Venue: Ad-Duha Institute, London

———————◆———————

Below is the text of 'Abd al-Qahir al-Baghdadi, *Kitab Usul al-Din*, pp.112-113 which outlines some views on the meaning of *"istiwa"* with his personal view given at the end.

المسألة الخامسة عشرة من هذا الأصل في معنى الاستواء المضاف اليه

اختلفوا في تأويل قوله تعالى: الرَّحْمَنُ عَلَى الْعَرْشِ اسْتَوَى، فزعمت المعتزلة انه بمعنى استولى كقول الشاعر: [قد] اسْتَوَى بِشْرٌ عَلَى الْعِرَاقِ اي استولى وهذا تأويل باطل لانه يوجب انه لم يكن مستوليا عليه قبل استوائه عليه. وزعمت المشبهة ان استواءه على العرش بمعنى كونه تماسا لعرشه من فوقه وابدت الكرامية لفظ الماسة بالملاقاة. وزعم بعضهم انه لا يفضل منه على العرش شيء [عن عرض العرش وهذا يوجب كونه في العرش على مقدار عرض العرش خ]. وزعم آخرون انه اكبر من العرش وانه لو خلق عن يمين العرش وعن يساره عرشين آخرين كان ملاقيا بجميعها من فوقها بلا واسطة وهذا يوجب ان يكون كل عرش كبعضه فيكون متبعضا. واختلف اصحابنا في هذا فمنهم من قال ان آية الاستواء من المتشابه الذي لا يعلم تأويله الا الله وهذا قول مالك بن انس وفقهاء

— ١١٣ —

المدينة والاصمعي. ورُويَ ان مالكا سُئلَ عن الاستواء فقال الاستواء معقول وكيفيته مجهولة والسؤال عنه بدعة والايمان به واجب. ومنهم من قال ان استواءه على العرش فعل احدثه في العرش سماه استواء كما احدث في بنيان قوم فعلا سماه اتيانا ولم يكن ذلك نزولا ولا حركة وهذا قول ابي الحسن الاشعري. ومنهم من قال ان استواءه على العرش كونه فوق العرش بلا مماسة وهذا قول القلانسي وعبدالله بن سعيد ذكره في كتاب الصفات. والصحيح عندنا تأويل العرش في هذه الآية على معنى الملك كأنه اراد ان الملك ما استوى لاحد غيره. وهذا التأويل

، خراسان. ومن تلامذة عبدالله بن سعيد ايضا شيخ به وامام الموحدين وله في التوحيد رسالة على شرط المتكلمين الصوفية. ثم بعدهم شيخ النظر وامام الآفاق في الجدل والتحقيق سن على بن اسماعيل الاشعري الذي صار شَجًا في حلوق القدرية [في كتاب التواريخ للمؤلف: كان ابن شريح ابدع الجماعة.

رية والجهمية والجسمية والروافض والخوارج وقد ملأ الدنيا وما رُزِقَ احد من المتكلمين من التَّبَع ما قد رُزِقَ لأن جميع اهل ث وكل من لم يتمزل من اهل الرأي على مذهبه. ومن تلامذته رين ابو الحسن الباهلي وابو عبدالله بن مجاهد وهما اللذان أتَمَرا هم الى اليوم شموسُ الزمانِ. وأئمة العصر كأبي بكر محمد طيب قاضي قضاة العراق والجزيرة وفارس وكرمان وساير حدود لنواحي. وابي بكر محمد بن الحسين بن فورك وابي اسحاق ابراهيم دالمهراني. وقبلهم ابوالحسن علي بن مهدي الطبري صاحب الفقه لم والاصول والادب والنحو والحديث. ومن آثاره تلميذ مثل دالله الحسين بن محمد البزازي صاحب الجدل والتصانيف في كل الكلام. وقبل هذه الطبقة شيخ العلوم [على الخصوص والعموم خ] الثقفي وفي زمانه كان امام اهل السنة ابو العباس القلانسي ادت تصانيفه في الكلام على مائة وخمسين كتابا. وتصانيف ونقوضه على اهل الاهواء زائدةٌ على مائة كتاب. وقد ادركنا عصرنا ابا عبدالله بن مجاهد ومحمد بن الطيب قاضي القضاة ن الحسين بن فورك وابراهيم بن محمد المهراني والحسين بن محمد، وعلى منوال هؤلاء الذين ادركناهم شيخُنا وهو لِاحْياءِ الحق كلٌّ وعلى اعدائه غُلٌّ.

Different Interpretations of "*istiwa*'" in the Asharite school:

View 1	View 2	View 3	View 4
It means "*istawla*":	It means literally with	It means a divine act:	It means above

'to conquer', 'to subdue' with resonances from Allah's attributes of 'al-Zahir', 'al-Qahhar', etc. > also, poetry of al-Akhtal for the linguistic origin:

قد استوى بشر على العراق/
من غير سيف ودم مهراق

And Bishr Conquered Iraq / without raising a sword or shedding blood
(= *Mukhtar al-Sihah*, p.136)

contact (*mumassah*): this is the literal reading that affirms Allah's contact with the Throne.

a created action that relates to the Throne but precludes movement and descent.

(*fawqa*) the Throne without any contact: i.e. it indicates 'aboveness' or 'highness' over the Throne but precludes any contact.

View 5: It refers to "mulk": Allah's exclusive power, dominion and sovereignty.

Below is an exegesis cluster of "*istiwa*'" according to the Asharite school. All readings of the Qur'anic ascription are valid in the school although scholars, over time, gave preference to one reading over that of another.

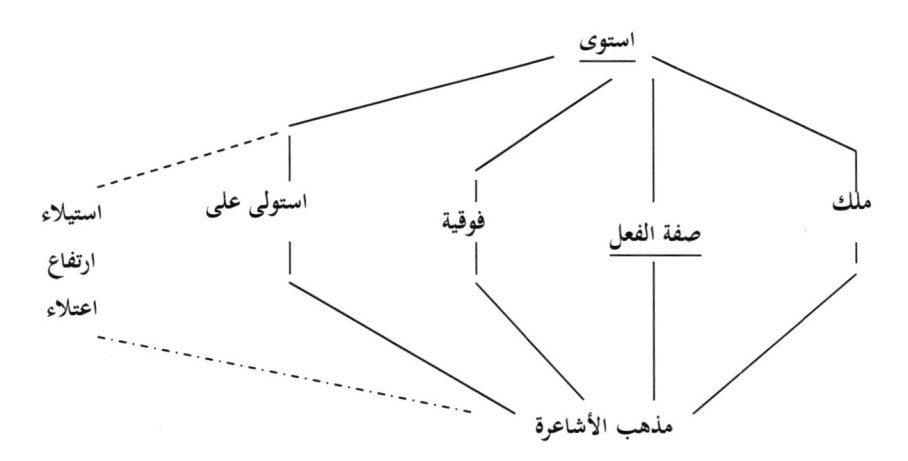

Fig.1. *Ta'wil* cluster of 'istiwa''

References: al-Bayhaqi, *al-Asma' wa'l-Sifat*, 2:308; Ibn Abi Ya'la, *al-Tabaqat al-Hanabilah*, 2:296-297; Ibn Hazm, *al-Fisal fi 'l-Milal*, 2:125; Ibn Hajar, *Fath al-Bari*, 13:409 and Ibn al-Qayyim, *al-Bada'i' al-Fawa'id*, 4:39-40

"*Sunnism* Side by Side: The Creed of the *Maqalat al-Islamiyyin*"

Course Module: 'Early Islamic Controversies'.
Topic: *early creed*.
Instructor: S. Z. Chowdhury
Venue: ad-Duha Institute, London.

———◆———

Below is a basic table of the differing approaches to the Hanbalite school as the position of al-Ash'ari and his adherents who formed the Ash'arite school of theology (cf. Handout on *Presuppositions*):

Hanbalite Position	The Ash'arite Position
• Essence-Attribute discussion is perilous and may lead to innovation	• Essence-Attribute discussion is meaningful and does not disrupt rational inquiry;
• Ontological status of attributes will remain concealed and the most than one can affirm is they exist because scripture states so although this does not preclude investigating their meanings for the believer.	• The principle of transcendence is not compromised by reasoned explications of the meanings behind divine attributes.
• Speculation is religious matters is not permitted as it is tantamount to linguistics, semantics and conceptual verbiage that leads to heresy or errors in faith.	• Theological inquiry is encouraged and although reason has its limits, it must be celebrated.

al-Ash'ari outlines in *Maqalat al-Islamiyyin*, vol.1, pp.320-325 the summary creedal statements of both *Ahl al-Sunnah* and the *Ahl al-Hadith*:

هذه حكاية جملة قول أصحاب الحديث وأهل السنة

جملة ما عليه أهل الحديث والسنة الإقرار بالله وملائكته وكتبه ورسله وما جاء من عند الله وما رواه الثقات عن رسول الله صلى الله عليه وسلم لا يردون من ذلك شيئاً وأن الله سبحانه إله واحد فرد صمد لا إله غيره لم يتخذ صاحبة ولا ولداً وأن محمداً عبده ورسوله وأن الجنة حق وأن النار حق وأن الساعة آتية لا ريب فيها وأن الله يبعث من في القبور.

وأن الله سبحانه على عرشه كما قال: "الرحمن على العرش استوى" وأن له يدين بلا كيف كما قال: "خلقت بيدي" وكما قال: "بل يداه مبسوطتان" وأن له عينين بلا كيف كما قال: "تجري بأعيننا" وأن له وجهاً كما قال: "ويبقى وجه ربك ذو الجلال والإكرام".

وأن أسماء الله لا يقال أنها غير الله كما قالت المعتزلة والخوارج وأقروا أن الله سبحانه علماً كما قال: "أنزله بعلمه" وكما قال: "وما تحمل من أنثى ولا تضع إلا بعلمه".

وأثبتوا السمع والبصر ولم ينفوا ذلك عن الله كما نفته المعتزلة وأثبتوا لله القوة كما قال: "أو لم يروا أن الله الذي خلقهم هو أشد منهم قوة". وقالوا أنه لا يكون في الأرض من خير ولا شر إلا ما شاء الله وأن الأشياء تكون بمشيئة الله كما قال عز وجل: "وما تشاؤون إلا أن يشاء الله" وكما قال المسلمون: ما شاء الله كان وما لا يشاء لا يكون.

وقالوا أن أحداً لا يستطيع أن يفعل شيئاً قبل أن يفعله أو يكون أحد يقدر أن يخرج عن علم الله أو أن يفعل شيئاً علم الله أنه لا يفعله وأقروا أنه لا خالق إلا الله وأن سيئات العباد يخلقها الله وأن أعمال العباد يخلقها الله عز وجل وأن العباد لا يقدرون أن يخلقوا شيئاً.

وأن الله سبحانه وفق المؤمنين لطاعته وخذل الكافرين ولطف بالمؤمنين ونظر لهم وأصلحهم وهداهم ولم يلطف بالكافرين ولا أصلحهم ولا هداهم ولو أصلحهم لكانوا صالحين ولو هداهم لكانوا مهتدين وأن الله سبحانه يقدر أن يصلح الكافرين ويلطف بهم حتى يكونوا مؤمنين ولكنه أراد أن لا يصلح الكافرين ويلطف بهم حتى يكونوا مؤمنين ولكنه أراد أن يكونوا كافرين كما علم وخذلهم وأضلهم وطبع على قلوبهم وأن الخير والشر بقضاء الله وقدره ويؤمنون بقضاء الله وقدره خيره وشره حلوه ومره ويؤمنون أنهم لا يملكون لأنفسهم نفعاً ولا ضراً إلا ما شاء الله كما قال ويلجئون أمرهم إلى الله سبحانه ويثبتون الحاجة إلى الله في كل وقت والفقر إلى الله في كل حال.

ويقولون أن القرآن كلام الله غير مخلوق والكلام في الوقف واللفظ من قال باللفظ أو بالوقف فهو مبتدع عندهم لا يقال اللفظ بالقرآن مخلوق ولا يقال غير مخلوق.

ويقولون أن الله سبحانه يرى بالأبصار يوم القيامة كما يرى القمر ليلة البدر يراه المؤمنون ولا يراه الكافرون لأنهم عن الله محجوبون قال الله عز وجل: "كلا إنهم عن ربهم يومئذ لمحجوبون" وأن موسى عليه السلام سأل الله سبحانه الرؤية في الدنيا وأن الله سبحانه تجلى للجبل فجعله دكاً فأعلمه بذلك أنه لا يراه في الدنيا بل يراه في الآخرة.

ولا يكفرون أحداً من أهل القبلة بذنب يرتكبه كنحو الزنا والسرقة وما أشبه ذلك من الكبائر وهم بما معهم من الإيمان مؤمنون وإن ارتكبوا الكبائر والإيمان عندهم هو الإيمان بالله وملائكته وكتبه ورسله وبالقدر خيره وشره حلوه ومره وأن ما أخطأهم لم يكن ليصيبهم وما أصابهم لم يكن ليخطئهم والإسلام هو أن يشهد أن لا إله إلا الله وأن محمداً رسول الله على ما جاء في الحديث والإسلام عندهم غير الإيمان.

ويقرون بأنه سبحانه مقلب القلوب.

ويقرون بشفاعة رسول الله صلى الله عليه وسلم وأنها لأهل الكبائر من أمته وبعذاب القبر وأن الحوض حق والصراط حق والبعث بعد الموت حق والمحاسبة من الله عز وجل للعباد حق والوقوف بين يدي الله حق.

ويقرون بأن الإيمان قول وعمل يزيد وينقص ولا يقولون مخلوق ولا غير مخلوق ويقولون: أسماء الله هي الله ولا يشهدون على أحد من أهل الكبائر ولا يحكمون بالجنة لأحد من الموحدين حتى يكون الله سبحانه ينزلهم حيث شاء ويقولون: أمرهم إلى الله إن شاء عذبهم وإن شاء غفر لهم ويؤمنون بأن الله سبحانه يخرج قوماً من الموحدين من النار على ما جاءت به الروايات عن رسول الله صلى الله عليه وسلم وينكرون الجدل والمراء في الدين والخصومة والمناظرة في القدر فيما يتناظر فيه أهل الجدل ويتنازعون فيه من دينهم بالتسليم للروايات الصحيحة ولما جاءت به الآثار التي رواها الثقات عدلاً عن عدل حتى ينتهي ذلك إلى رسول الله صلى الله عليه وسلم ولا يقولون كيف ولا لم لأن ذلك بدعة.

ويقولون أن الله لم يأمر بالشر بل نهى عنه وأمر بالخير ولم يرض بالشر وإن كان مريداً له.

ويعرفون حق السلف الذين اختارهم الله سبحانه لصحبة نبيه صلى الله عليه وسلم ويأخذون بفضائلهم ويمسكون عما شجر بينهم صغيرهم وكبيرهم ويقدمون أبا بكر ثم عمر ثم عثمان ثم علياً رضوان الله عليهم ويقرون أنهم الخلفاء الراشدون المهديون أفضل الناس كلهم بعد النبي صلى الله عليه وسلم.

ويصدقون بالأحاديث التي جاءت عن رسول الله صلى الله عليه وسلم أن الله سبحانه ينزل إلى السماء الدنيا فيقول هل من مستغفر كما جاء الحديث عن رسول الله صلى الله عليه وسلم ويأخذون بالكتاب والسنة كما قال الله عز وجل: " <u>فإن تنازعتم في شيء فردوه إلى الله والرسول</u> " ويرون اتباع من سلف من أئمة الدين وأن لا يبتدعوا في دينهم ما لم يأذن به الله.

ويقرون أن الله سبحانه يجيء يوم القيامة كما قال: " <u>وجاء ربك والملك صفاً صفاً</u> " وأن الله يقرب من خلقه كيف يشاء كما قال: " <u>ونحن أقرب إليه من حبل الوريد</u> ".

ويرون العيد والجمعة والجماعة خلف كل إمام بر وفاجر ويثبتون المسح على الخفين سنة ويرونه في الحضر والسفر ويثبتون فرض الجهاد للمشركين منذ بعث الله نبيه صلى الله عليه وسلم إلى آخر عصابة تقاتل الدجال وبعد ذلك.

ويرون الدعاء لأيمة المسلمين بالصلاح وأن لا يخرجوا عليهم بالسيف وأن لا يقاتلوا في الفتنة ويصدقون بخروج الدجال وأن عيسى بن مريم يقتله.

ويؤمنون بمنكر ونكير والمعراج والرؤيا في المنام وأن الدعاء لموتى المسلمين والصدقة عنهم بعد موتهم تصل إليهم.

ويصدقون بأن في الدنيا سحرة وأن الساحر كافر كما قال الله وأن السحر كائن موجود في الدنيا.

ويرون الصلاة على كل من مات من أهل القبلة برهم وفاجرهم وموارثتهم.

ويقرون أن الجنة والنار مخلوقتان.

وأن من مات مات بأجله وكذلك من قتل قتل بأجله.

وأن الأرزاق من قبل الله سبحانه يرزقها عباده حلالاً كانت أم حراماً وأن الشيطان يوسوس للإنسان ويشككه ويخبطه.

وأن الصالحين قد يجوز أن يخصهم الله بآيات تظهر عليهم.

وأن السنة لا تنسخ بالقرآن.

وأن الأطفال أمرهم إلى الله إن شاء عذبهم وإن شاء فعل بهم ما أراد وأن الله عالم بالعباد عاملون وكتب أن ذلك يكون وأن الأمور بيد الله ويرون الصبر على حكم الله والأخذ بما أمر الله به والانتهاء عما نهى الله عنه وإخلاص العمل والنصيحة للمسلمين ويدينون بعبادة الله في العابدين والنصيحة لجماعة المسلمين واجتناب الكبائر والزنا وقول الزور والعصبية والفخر والكبر والإزراء على الناس والعجب.

ويرون مجانبة كل داع إلى بدعة والتشاغل بقراءة القرآن وكتابة الآثار والنظر في الفقه مع التواضع والاستكانة وحسن الخلق وبذل المعروف وكف الأذى وترك الغيبة والنميمة والسعاية وتفقد المأكل والمشرب.

فهذه جملة ما يأمرون به ويستعملونه ويرونه وبكل ما ذكرنا من قولهم نقول وإليه نذهب وما توفيقنا إلا بالله وهو حسبنا ونعم الوكيل وبه نستعين وعليه نتوكل وإليه المصير.

Notes:

- There are no official creeds in Islam but there are catalogues of key doctrines.

- Creedal works were often written for instructional purposes.
- Articles listed in the creeds contain matters not related to doctrine but had doctrinal implications.

- Textual features:

1. It is in effect a creedal work listing what Muslims believe and assent to.

2. Note the terms *"yu'minun"* ('they believe with absolute certainty'), *"yusaddiquna"* ('they affirm') and *"yarawna"* ('they hold', 'they see as', 'they view…').

3. al-Ash'ari delineates the same creed of the People of *Sunnah* (Ash'arite *Mutakallimun*) and the People of *Hadith* (scripturalist theologians).

4. It is a short list of contentious theological issues up until the early 4th / 10th centuries that have created sectarian divisions but al-Ash'ari presents a unified conservative creed across the *sunni* Islamic spectrum.

- The creedal subject matters mentioned in the text include:

1. Affirming the unity of Allah.
2. Affirming the veracity of the Prophet's career.
3. Affirming the reality of heaven and hell.
4. Affirming divine ascriptions such as 'face', 'hands', 'eyes', etc. and not deny them like the Mu'tazilites did.
5. To affirm the attributes are not distinct from Allah and not deny such attributes as 'knowledge' and 'power' as well as 'sight' and 'hearing' mentioned in the Qur'an like the Mu'tazilites did.
6. No-one can escape the knowledge of Allah.
7. Allah creates the actions of human beings.
8. Allah has commanded obedience from the believers.
9. Allah has shown clemency to the believers and reserves humiliation for the non-believers but has the power to reverse that.
10. Good and evil are in the decree of Allah and does not occur outside His Will.
11. The Qur'an is not created.
12. Affirming the beatific vision (*visio dei*) in the hereafter.
13. Committing sins does not cause one to become a disbeliever.
14. Allah can change the conditions of peoples' hearts.
15. Islam comprises of the profession of faith (*shahadah*).
16. What was meant to hit you will and what was not, will not.
17. The Prophetic intercession is a reality.
18. Punishment in the grave is a reality.

19. Resurrection is a reality.
20. Standing before Allah is a reality.
21. Events and places of the hereafter are real.
22. Belief consists of statements and actions and can increase and decrease.
23. Judgments on the fate of peoples are ultimately for Allah.
24. Condemnation of theological disputation over the Divine decree and the nature of the Qur'an and inquiry into matters of the Divine attributes.
25. Forgiving is a contingent act of divine mercy.
26. Allah's 'coming' and 'nearness' are mentioned in the text and affirmed as they have been stated.
27. The rightly guided caliphs in order of excellence and rank – without diminishing anything from other companions of the Prophet – are Abu Bakr, 'Umar, 'Uthman and 'Ali and they are the best of people after the Prophets.
28. The Companions are the best of people chosen by Allah and have rights.
29. The generation of the *salaf* are emulated, followed and taken as an example.
30. The righteous scholars of this religion are followed.
31. The Friday Prayer as well as the two Eid Prayers are valid behind a righteous and impious Imam.
32. Wiping over leather footgear is an established practice of the Prophet (*sunnah*).
33. Jihad is an obligation until end of time.
34. The Dajjal will emerge and be slain by Prophet Jesus, the Messiah.
35. It is not permitted to take up arms against the legitimate rulers.
36. The Angels Munkar and Nakir are real.
37. Supplications for the deceased as well as any rewards from works of charity reach them.
38. The Heavenly journey (*mi'raj*) is real.
39. Magic is real and the one engaged in it has disbelieved.
40. Heaven and Hell are created.
41. When one dies, it is because his life-term (*ajal*) has expired.
42. All sustenance is from Allah and set by Him and it is human beings that unlock this sustenance due to Satanic insinuations.
43. The righteous servants of Allah can be granted signs to manifest the truth.
44. The fate of children ultimately lies with Allah; if He wishes he may treat them favourably or vice-versa.
45. Attitudinal matters are upheld such as humility when studying the traditions or religious books; good character; to have patience when adhering to the rulings of Allah; to have sincerity in actions; to counsel one another; to avoid major sins and internal faults associated with the ego.

References: al-Ash'ari's *al-Ibanah 'an Usul al-Diyanah, Kitab al-Luma', Istihsan al-Khawd fi 'Ilm al-Kalam* (= cf. Rev. R. J. McCarthy, *The Theology of al-Ash'ari*). See also A. J.

Wensinck, §§'Fikh al-Akbar I', 'Fikh al-Akbar II' in *The Muslim Creed*; the notes in W. M. Watt, *Islamic Creeds: A Selection* and the translator's notes in al-Taftazani's commentary of Najm al-Din al-Nasafi's text on Islamic creed translated by E. E. Elder as *A Commentary on the Creed of Islam*.

Part Four: *Free Will*

 2. Hellenistic Background.
F. Part 1: Origins of the Controversy.
G. Part 2: Meaning of the Terms *Qada'* and *Qadar*.
H. Part 3: Revisiting *Qada'* and *Qadar*.
I. Part 4: Conclusions.
J. Part 5: al-Ash'ari and the Theory of *Kasb*.

Background

"The Ol' Problem from Antiquity: *The Greeks and Free Will Discussions*"

Course Module: 'Early Islamic Controversies'.
Topic: *background reading free will*.
Instructor: S. Z. Chowdhury
Venue: ad-Duha Institute, London.

———◆———

- Below are just some of the views from materialist pre-Socratic philosophers on free will and determinism which later led Socrates, Plato, Aristotle and the Pythagoreans with later post-Aristotelian philosophers to further elaborate on the discussion. Finally, these thoughts found their entry into early Islamic polemics through the first wave of Hellenism transmitted through the Greek-Arabic translation movement and Muslim interaction of ideas with other theological traditions.

General Context:

1. The need for human *responsibility* in order to justify human *accountability*.
2. The need to originate human action from within the person (human *agency* is linked to human *capacity*).
3. Choice is linked to accountability and is 'what comes from us' ([Gr. ἐφ ἡμῖν] = 'free will').
4. Fate (everything has been fixed the way it was, is and will be).
5. Freedom from arbitrary control of man's fate by the gods.
6. Laws (λόγος) govern the physical world (φύσις) and order it by necessity.

[1] **Pre-Socratics**:

View 1 – Leucippus

"Nothing occurs at random (μάτην), but everything for a reason (λόγου) and by necessity."

Οὐδὲν χρῆμα μάτην γίνεται, ἀλλὰ πάντα ἐκ λόγου τε καὶ ὑπ' ἀνάγκης

View 2 – Democritus

"By convention (νόμῳ) color, by convention sweet, by convention bitter, but in reality atoms and a void."

Νόμῳ χροιή, νόμῳ γλυκύ, νόμῳ πικρόν, ἐτεῇ δ' ἄτομα καὶ κενόν

- Absolute necessity.
- Dogmatic determinist universe.
- No possibility for chance.
- An atomic component of cosmology meant the motion of atoms was causally determined.

- These views resulted in a kind of *material determinism* (i.e. our actions being caused by the laws of cause and effect without any choice) and if this is the case then there can only be one future and one possibility or outcome. Thus, we are not really free but have the *illusion* of freedom.

[2] **Aristotle**:

- Aristotle wanted to argue that virtue and vice was acquired through voluntary actions. He also wanted to argue that human accountability, praise and blame and moral responsibility were linked with human choice.

- For Aristotle, there was no absolute mechanistic nexus of cause and effect, i.e. for every effect there had to be a prior temporal cause but he also posited something indeterminate (ἀόριστον) like 'chance' (τυχόν) being a cause of things as well.

- Aristotelian scholars know too well the lack of clarity in his formulation on the topic of human capacity for choice. Nevertheless, put basically, Aristotle argued that for an action (or indeed internal states, thinking patterns and reasoning) to be originated within a person, it depends on whether or not the person desires or wants to do it. Thus, the origin (ἀρχῆ) of the action is the agent himself.

[3] **Epicurus**:

- For Epicurus, chance and necessity both destroy human choice and hence human responsibility. He argued that praise and blame can only be connected to free actions, i.e. human agency.
- He argued that there was a *tertium quid* (some 'third thing') beyond necessity in the physical world (φύσις) and chance (τυχόν) and this third thing was human agency or power to choose:

A. "[...] some things happen of necessity (ἀνάγκη), others by chance (τύχη), others through our own agency (παρ' ἡμᾶς)."

B. "[...] necessity destroys responsibility and chance is inconstant; whereas our own actions are autonomous, and it is to them that praise and blame naturally attach."

- A. A. Long and D. N. Sedley state:

   Epicurus' problem is this: if it has been necessary all along that we should act as we do, it cannot be up to us, with the result that we would not be morally responsible for our actions at all. Thus posing the problem of determinism he becomes arguably the first philosopher to recognize the philosophical centrality of what we know as the Free Will Question. His strongly libertarian approach to it can be usefully contrasted with the Stoics' acceptance of determinism.

[3] **Chrysippus**:

- Chrysippus was looking to find a way of disconnecting external causes that 'make us' do our actions and move to a link to human agency and choice from 'within'. This led to an early form of **compatibilism** between determinism and free will.

- He argued that the cosmos or the physical world was governed by an unalterable fate or determined way things will be. He also argued that everything has a prior cause for it and so there was no room in the causal nexus of things for chance. But if there is no room for chance or change and everything is determined, where does human choice fit in? Chrysippus states that the way we can enter the causal chain of determined events is our power/capacity/ability to decide how to *react* to or *assent* to what we experience or sense. This power/capacity comes from *our own nature* (from 'within us' / 'ἐφ ἡμῖν') and not externally caused by someone or something out there. By mere virtue of this fact, we exercise choice and responsibility from our own selves despite an externally caused world. (cf. Chrysippus' simile of the rolling cylinder).

References: Diels Kranz, *Die Fragmente der Vorsokratiker*, Fragment B125; Leucippus, Fragment 569 - from Fr. 2 Actius I, 25, 4; Epicurus, *Letter to Menoeceus*, §133; Long and Sedley, *The Hellenistic Philosophers*, §20, "Free Will," p.107 and E. Eliasson, *The Notion of That Which Depends on Us in Plotinus and its Background*, pp.47-61 (Aristotle) and 81-97 (Chrysippus).

"Part 1: The Origins of the Free Will Controversy"

Course: 'Early Islamic Controversies'
Topic: *qada' and qadar outlines*
Instructor: S. Z. Chowdhury
Venue: Ad-Duha Institute, London

———◆———

§1. Context and Survey of Early Views

Below is a basic schema for the context surrounding the free will controversy in early Islamic history. It also outlines the stages of the development of the doctrine up until al-Ash'ari during the 4th / 10th century.

[1] 650-750: *emergence of proto-libertarian views*

Pre-Islamic fatalism: large element of fatalism in Arabian society; human life is controlled by time (*dahr*; *zaman*) and man must just submit to the vicissitudes of time as it is futile to try and change what is and will be; primarily, the *outcome* of man's acts are determined and fixed not the act themselves.

⬇

| الدهر ‖ 'Time' that affects everyone and is inescapable |

Umayyad claims of Divine right: Their appointment as political leaders (especially the Marwanid Branch r. 684-750) was argued as being Allah's bestowal and denial of it is tantamount to countering Allah's wisdom and determination. Also, it is a duty on all Muslims to obey their leader (*amir*) and refusal is a major sin.

Allah chose the Umayyads to be

⬇

Obedience therefore is necessary

Qur'anic data: There are plenty of verse that mention qualities of Allah that point to a power beyond human beings and the acts, e.g.

- Allah as 'al-Qadir'.
- Allah as 'al-Khabir'.
- Allah as 'al-Muqtadir'.

Qur'anic precepts also point towards an overpowering force that governs and determines human history and events, e.g.

- *Rizq*: sustenance is fixed and unalterable;
- *Ajal*: life span is fixed and unalterable.
- *Lawh al-mahfuz*: 'the prescribed tablet' on which information of everything is written.

From the close of the first century and the beginning of the second century there emerged opposition to prevailing ideas of predestination with bold claims of direct free will and human agency; views which became the precursors to later theological articulation within a *kalam* framework by Mu'tazlite thinkers:

Ma'bad al-Juhani (c. 80/704)	**Ghaylan al-Dimashqi** (d. 125/743)	**Kharijite Movement** (660-750)
Little is known about him; his views are said to be derived from a Christian heretic; his formulation of qadarite doctrine are unclear. He argued that acts of human beings were free – especially morally unjust ones and that the injustices of the Umayyad ruling class were not determined by Allah.	Possibly a Coptic Christian who had a position as secretary in the Umayyad administration; he accounted various Umayyad rulers urging them to avoid stoicism and alter policies and was sternly reprimanded as a result; He believed Allah did not determine evil actions (justified by political powers) and that human agency was positive; he also believed that a non-Qurashite individual could be appointed to the office of the Caliphate as long as he ruled by the Qur'an and Sunnah; he upheld that actions were not part of belief (*iman*) and that belief neither increased nor decreased; he also believed that knowledge was of two types: *necessary* (primary) and *acquired* (secondary);	Early kharijites of Basra were documented to have held qadarite views; their insistence on moral earnestness as well as Allah's justice naturally aligned them to libertarian views.

- Some of the early <u>determinist</u> views from *kalam* discussions include the following:

Jahm Ibn Safwan (d. 128/745)	**Early Determinist Sects** (700-850)

Arabic text: al-Ash'ari, *al-maqalat al-Islamiyyin*, p.279:

"Jahm [Ibn Safwan] alone held the following opinions: that Heaven and Hell will begin and perish; that *iman* is knowledge of Allah only and *kufr* is ignorance of Him; that humans do not in reality act only Allah does – Allah alone is the 'doer' whereas human beings are attributed with acting in a metaphorical sense, e.g. as in when it is said 'a tree moves' or the 'spheres rotate' or 'the sun rises'. It is really Allah who acts through them. Moreover, humans are created with a power (*quwwah*) to act as well as a unique will and choice to act in the same way Allah has made him with a height by which he is tall and a colouring by which he has colour"

الذى تفرد به جهم القول بأن الجنة والنار تبيدان وتفنيان وأن الإيمان هو المعرفة بالله فقط والكفر هو الجهل به فقط وأنه لا فعل لأحد في الحقيقة إلا الله وحده وأنه هو الفاعل وأن الناس إنما تنسب إليهم أفعالهم على المجاز كما يقال تحركت الشجرة ودار الفلك وزالت الشمس وإنما فعل ذلك بالشجرة والفلك والشمس سبحانه الله إلا أنه خلق للإنسان قوة كان بها الفعل وخلق له إرادة للفعل واختيارا له منفردا به بذلك كما خلق له طولا كان به طويلا ولونا كان به متلونا

Arabic text: al-Qurtubi, *al-Jami' li-Ahkam al-Qur'an*, 4:163:

"The Jabriyyah divide into twelve sects that include: [1] the Mudtarriyyah who held the view that humans do not really act but only Allah acts everything; then there is [2] the Af'aliyyah who said that we do act but we do not actually have the capacity to act; we are like animals tied and led on a rope; [3] the Mafrughiyyah believe that everything is already created [s: beforehand] and that nothing now is created; [4] the Najjariyyah alleged that Allah Most High punishes people because of what He does and not because of what *they* do; [5] the Mannaniyyah said: 'Whatever occurs in your heart then that is upon you so do whatever good has been already written for you'; [6] the Kasbiyyah say that a person does not acquire any reward or punishment; [7] the Sabiqiyyah say: whoever wants, let them act and whoever does not then let them not because the saved and felicitous will not be harmed by their sins and the damned will not be benefited by their piety […]"

الجبرية

اثنتي عشرة فرقة:

فمنهم المضطرية – قالوا: لا فعل للآدمي، بل الله يفعل الكل. والأفعالية – قالوا: لنا أفعال ولكن لا استطاعة لنا فيها، وإنما نحن كالبهائم نقاد بالحبل. والمفروغية – قالوا: كل الأشياء قد خلقت، والآن لا يخلق شيء. والنجارية – زعمت أن الله تعالى يعذب الناس على فعله لا على فعلهم. والمنانية – قالوا: عليك بما يخطر بقلبك، فافعل ما توسمت منه الخير. والكسبية – قالوا: لا يكتسب العبد ثوابا ولا عقابا. والسابقية – قالوا: من شاء فليعمل ومن شاء فلا يعمل، فإن السعيد لا تضره ذنوبه والشقي لا ينفعه بره. والحِبية – قالوا: من شرب كأس محبة الله تعالى سقطت عنه عبادة الأركان. والخوفية – قالوا: من أحب الله تعالى لم يسعه أن يخافه، لأن الحبيب لا يخاف حبيبه. والفكرية – قالوا: من ازداد علما أسقط عنه بقدر ذلك من العبادة. والخشبية – قالوا: الدنيا بين العباد سواء، لا تفاضل بينهم فيما ورثهم أبوهم آدم. والمنية – قالوا: منا الفعل ولنا الاستطاعة.

Thus, on the determinist view, we have:

1. Allah has determined all things – including human actions.
2. Human beings do not really act but only metaphorically.
3. Acts as well as their effects are also created by Allah.
4. Nothing can change what is already written for someone so actions are futile.

- Some of the early <u>libertarian</u> views from *kalam* discussions include the following:

Wasil Ibn 'Ata' **(d. 131/748)**	**Early Rationalist Views** **(700-850)**
Arabic Text: al-Shahrastani, *al-Milal*, p.32.	**Arabic Text:** al-Malati's *Kitab al-Tanbih*, 1:74-77:
"He held that the Creator Most High is Wise and Just and it is not permitted to ascribe evil and injustice to Him. It is also not possible that He wills of His servant to act contrary to what He has commanded him and it is equally not possible that He decrees something for His servant and then recompenses him for it. It is the servant who is the doer of good and bad, belief and disbelief, obedience and disobedience and it is metaphorically ascribed to him whereas the Lord Most High is the one who gives him the ability to be able to do all of it…"	"One of the groups of the qadariyyah called the 'mufawwida' believed they have been entrusted or devolved the ability to do good without the grace or guidance of Allah […] another group held that Allah created in man the complete capacity [s: to freely act] that needs no increase so man has the capacity to believe, disbelieve, eat, drink, stand, sit, sleep and wake up and do whatever he wishes. They also held that man is able to believe because if that were not the case then they would have been punished by Allah for something they were not capable of doing […] another group called the Shabibiyyah also denied that Allah's knowledge is antecedent to what man does and what they become […]"
فقال إن الباري تعالى حكيم عادل لا يجوز أن يضاف إليه شر ولا ظلم ولا يجوز أن يريد من العباد خلاف ما يأمر ويحتم عليهم شيئاً ثم يجازيهم عليه فالعبد هو الفاعل للخير والشر والإيمان والكفر والطاعة والمعصية وهو المجازى على فعله والرب تعالى أقدره على ذلك كله.	ومن القدرية صنف يقال لهم المفوضة زعموا أنهم موكلون إلى أنفسهم إنهم يقدرون على الخير كله بالتفويض الذي يذكرون دون توفيق الله وهداه … ومنهم صنف زعموا أن الله عز و جل جعل إليهم الاستطاعة تاما كاملا لا يحتاجون إلى أن يزدادوا فيه فاستطاعوا أن يؤمنوا وأن يكفروا ويأكلوا ويشربوا ويقوموا ويقعدوا ويرقدوا ويستيقظوا وأن يعملوا ما أرادوا وزعموا أن العباد كانوا يستطيعون أن يؤمنوا ولولا ذلك ما عذبهم على مالا يستطيعون إليه … ومنهم صنف شبيبية فهؤلاء أيضا أنكروا أن يكون العلم سابقا على

ما به العباد عاملون وما هم إليه صائرون ... ومنهم صنف أنكروا أن الله عز و جل خلق ولد الزنا أو قدره أو شاءه أو علمه تعالى الله عما قالوا وأنكروا أن يكون الرجل الذي سرق في عمره كله أو يأكل الحرام أن يكون ذلك رزق الله عز و جل وقالوا لم يرزقه الله رزقا قط إلا حلالا ... ومنهم صنف زعموا أن الله عز و جل وقت لهم الأرزاق والآجال لوقت معلوم فمن قتل قتيلا فقد أعجله عن أجله ورزقه لغير أجله وبقي له من الرزق ما لم يستوفه ولم يستكمله

Thus on the libertarian view we have:

1. Allah creates a capacity for human beings to act freely.
2. Human beings have full control and power to act freely.
3. Allah's knowledge is not chronologically prior to someone acting and so does not cause it.
4. No evil is to be ascribed to Allah only to human action.

[2] 750-900: *Early Mu'tazilite Kalam views*

The discussion of free will and determinism (*al-ikhtiyar wa 'l-jabr*) as entertained by the Mu'tazilite *Mutakallimun* as well as theologians of the $2^{nd} - 5^{th} / 8^{th} - 10^{th}$ centuries were built on the earlier intimations and discussions connected to the political contexts in which they emerged but were framed within a context that was rooted in antiquity (i.e. the Hellenised world [cf. the handout on *Kalam* and its development]). Essentially, the concept of '*qadar*' and its sister term '*qada*'' took on a deeply scholastic tenor and given a technical meaning that the scriptural data did not bear. In other words, an essentially rational discussion was weaved into the text of the Qur'an to support a debate that had no bearing on the philological meanings of the text. This gave rise to the controversy of 'free will' (*al-ikhtiyar*) and 'compulsion' (*al-jabr*) as well as whether 'man's actions' (*af'al al-'ibad*) are created or not. A number of related issues were discussed in a technical way by Mu'tazilite thinkers that formed the basis of the discussion on free will and determinism which has – in reality – no connection to the matter of *al-qada' wa 'l-qadar* (also refer to the part 2 and part 3 of the handouts). The issues include

1. *Divine justice and human free choice*: Allah cannot do injustice/evil or be ascribed with injustice/evil; Allah's character is essentially Good and so always does what is best for them [= the doctrine of *islah*]; evil/injustice is the product from human agency and choice, etc. ⟶ **driven by the principle of Divine unity, transcendence and justice**.

2. *Whether Allah's knowledge determines human actions*: Divine foreknowledge appears to preclude human agency; if foreknowledge precludes freedom then it renders choice meaningless. ⎯⎯⎯→ **driven by the principle of Divine unity, transcendence, justice and human responsibility.**

3. *Whether Allah creates man's action and its effects or not*: do humans originate or produce their own action and their effects? Can 'creating' only properly be ascribed to Allah? Is action a determined entity of creation? If humans are not originators of their own action then human choice and moral freedom is essentially meaningless. ⎯⎯⎯→ **driven by the moral accountability and human responsibility.**

[3] 900-1050: *Theories of 'kasb' and formation of 'Orthodoxy'.*

(Refer to the handout on al-Maturidi's theory of *kasb* as well as al-Ash'ari's formulation below)

References: D. Gimaret, "Mu'tazila", in *EI²*, 7:783-93; Wolfson, *The Philosophy of the Kalam*, pp.601-719; G. Endress, *Islam: An Historical Introduction*, pp.43-51 and Watt, *The Formative Period of Islamic Thought*, pp.82-118.

"Part 2:
The Meanings of *Qada'* and Qadar"

Course: 'Early Islamic Controversies'
Topic: *meanings of qada' and qadar*
Instructor: S. Z. Chowdhury
Venue: Ad-Duha Institute, London

- The linguistic meanings of *qadar* include:

QADAR

Linguistic Meanings

1. (دبر) *dabbara shay'an*/to organise, arrange…	2. (هيئ) *hayya'a shay'an*/to fix, put in order, arrange…	3. (وقت) *waqqata shay'an*/to fix and appoint…
4. (قدر) *qaddara lahu al-amra*/to decide a matter, judge a matter…	5. (قسم) *qassama rizaqahu*/to determine the sustenance of s.th/s.o…	6. (ضيق) *dayyaqa*/to limit and restrict…

- The Qur'anic meanings include:

QADAR

Qur'anic Meanings

1. 33:38 (*The Command of Allah is a <u>decree determined</u> [qadaran maqdura]…*) = a strong, established, firm, inescapable and definitive command or matter.

2. 89:16 (*and when He tries him by <u>straitening out his means of life</u> [fa-qadara 'alayhi rizqahu]…*) = tightening, limiting, and restricting the provision or means.

3. 5:12 (*…so the waters [of the heavens and the earth met for <u>a matter predestined</u> [amrin qad qudira]…]*) = an event determined by Allah in the *Lawh al-Mahfuz* ('Divine

Tablet'), viz. the destruction of Nuh's people by the flood.

4. 41:10 (...*and <u>measured therein its sustenance</u> [wa qaddara fiha aqwataha]*...) = put in it vegetation or food for the people.

5. 74:18 (*verily, he pondered and <u>plotted</u> [fakkara wa qaddara]*...) = pondering over what is said in the Qur'an and what his soul makes him do.

6. 92:7 (*... Who has created and then proportioned it; Who <u>has measured and the guided</u> [walladhi qaddara fa hada]*...) = he has measured and given all that improves and is beneficial for animals which they are made to recognise, i.e. given them needs that have to satisfy.

7. 34:18 (*...and <u>we made the stages easy</u> [qaddarna fiha al-sayr]*...) = making it safe and sound.

8. (*And Allah has <u>set a measure</u> [qadran] for all things*...) = i.e. an appointment and measure.

9. 15:21 (*and we send it not down but in <u>a known measure</u> [bi-qadrin ma'lumin]*) = a known time.

10. (*We have created all things with a <u>Divine pre-ordainment</u> [bi-qadrin]*...) = pre-determined.

11. 56:60 (*We have <u>decreed</u> [qaddarna] death to you all and we are not outstripped*...) = we have determined the phenomena of death as well as the differences in ages and lifespan.

12. 20:40 (*you came here <u>according to</u> ['ala qadrin] a time I ordained O Musa*...) = a designated time.

13. 15:60 (*except his wife whom <u>We determined</u> [qaddarna] should of those who remain behind*...) = i.e. decided it to be so.

- From the *ahadith*, we have some of the following narrations mentioning the meaning of *qadar*:

A. "…she has whatever is determined (destined) for her…"[18] – meaning whatever is written in the *lawh al-mahfuz* and hence what Allah knows.

لا تسأل المرأة طلاق أختها لتستفرغ صحفتها ، ولتنكح، فإن لها ما قدر لها…

B. "…to the time determined for him…"[19]

Here, *qadr* takes the meaning of destined, fixed, decreed and ordained (*taqdir*) as well as Allah's knowledge.

لا يأتي ابن آدم النذر بشيء لم يكن قدر له، ولكن يلقيه النذر إلى القدر قد قدر له، فيستخرج الله به من البخيل، فيؤتيني عليه ما لم يكن يؤتيني عليه من قبل…

C. "…a matter determined before I was created…" – meaning 'written' (*kutiba*), i.e. Allah's knowledge of it which is by the effect of God's pre-ordainment/decree of it in the *lawh al-mahfuz*.

احتج آدم وموسى ، فقال له موسى : أنت آدم الذي أخرجتك خطيئتك من الجنة، فقال له آدم : أنت موسى الذي اصطفاك برسالاته وبكلامه، ثم تلومني على أمر قدر علي قبل أن أخلق . فقال رسول الله صلى الله عليه وسلم : فحج آدم موسى . مرتين.

D. "Everything is determined; even powerlessness and intelligence or intelligence and powerlessness"[20] – meaning everything things is fixed and determined by Allah and that He knows it, i.e. He has written it in the *lawh al-mahfuz*.

عن طاوس اليماني أنه قال : أدركت ناسا من أصحاب النبي صلى الله عليه وسلم يقولون : كل شيء بقدر . قال طاوس : وسمعت عبد الله بن عمر يقول : قال رسول الله صلى الله عليه وسلم : كل شيء بقدر , حتى العجز و الكيس ,أو الكيس و العجز.

---

[18] Bukhari, *Sahih* (§6601).
[19] Bukhari, *Sahih* (§6694).
[20] Muslim, *Sahih* (§2655) and Ibn 'Abd al-Barr, *al-Tamhid*, 6:62 and his *al-Istidhkar*, 7:269 stating that the *isnad* ('chain of transmission') is *sahih* ('sound').

"...when matters pertaining to *al-qadr* is mentioned, hold fast on to it..."[21] – meaning if the *taqdir* and Knowledge of Allah is mentioned, then do not quarrel over it because it is to do with the Attribute of Allah that he is Omniscient; hence believe in it and submit to it.

إذا ذكر القدر فأمسكوا...

"...instead, say, 'Allah determined it and what he willed I did'..."[22] – meaning what Allah wrote it down in the *lawh al-mahfuz*, i.e. His knowledge. This is pertaining to Allah's knowledge and does not enter into the discussion of *al-qada' wa 'l-qadar*.

المؤمن القوي خير وأحب إلى الله من المؤمن الضعيف . وفي كل خير . احرص على ما ينفعك واستعن بالله . ولا تعجز . وإن أصابك شيء فلا تقل : لو أني فعلت كان كذا وكذا . ولكن قل : قدر الله . وما شاء فعل . فإن لو تفتح عمل الشيطان...

- From all these different meanings above from both the linguistic and textual sources, there is no meaning that pertains to that as defined by the scholastics (*al-mutakallimun*), viz. the actions of human beings and whether they were created or not.

- All the meanings for *qadar* as given in the Qur'an and the hadith refer to Allah's pre-ordainment (*taqdiruhu*) and His knowledge, i.e. Allah's writing of it in the *lawh al-mahfuz* which refers to His knowledge (*'ilmuhu*).[23]

---

[21] Mentioned by al-Hafiz Ibn Hajar al-'Asqalani in *Fath al-Bari Sharh Sahih al-Bukhari*,11:476 declaring the *isnad* as *hasan* ('good') and al-Haythami, *Majma' al-Zawa'id*, 7:205. Another version as graded *hasan* by al-'Iraqi in *al-Mughni 'an al-Asfar fi 'l-Asfar*, 1:50 (= *takhrij* ['sourcing'] of the hadiths in *Ihya'* of al-Ghazzali), has:

"If my Companions are mentioned to you, hold fast onto them; when the stars are mentioned, follow them and when *al-qadr* is mentioned, accept it".

إذا ذكر أصحابي فأمسكوا وإذا ذكر النجوم فأمسكوا وإذا ذكر القدر فأمسكوا...

[22] Muslim, *Sahih* (§2664).
[23] The *lawh al-mahfuz* is the symbolic representation of Allah's knowledge and will. See al-Nabhani, *Nizam al-Islam*, p.31.

- These terms are used in their *linguistic* sense and hence cannot be rationalised (especially from a Hellenised context). If there is no *shar'i*-meaning discernible from the texts/sources (i.e. Qur'an and hadith), then a term that is given a technical definition cannot then be said to take on a *shar'i*-meaning.

§2. AL-QADA'

- Again, the discussion over *qada'* is equally complex.
- The term has a number of linguistic usages:

QADA'

Linguistic Meanings

1. (أبرم) *abrama shay'an*/to decree and decide upon…

2. (قدر) *qaddara sha'yan*/to decree and determine s.th…

3. (صنع) *sana'a shay'an*/to create, fashion and make s.th…

4. (تم) *yutimmu shay'an*/to conclude, complete and bring to an end successfully…

5. (أهلك) *ahlaka shay'an*/to exterminate, destroy and annihilate…

- There are also a number of Qur'anic meanings:

QADA'

Qur'anic Meanings

1. 2:117 (***When He decrees something [idha qada amran], He says only, 'Be!' and it is***) = meaning when Allah establishes or confirms something, then it unfailingly comes into existence. Cf. also 8:42 (*so

2. (***He is the one who created you all from clay and decreed your lifespan***) = meaning Allah is the one who has made everyone from clay and then determined the lifespan (*ajalan*) i.e. the duration

3. 41:12 (***He fashioned them [qadahunna] as seven heavens…***) = meaning Allah created the heavens in their seven states and levels.

Allah may <u>bring about a matter that is ordained</u> [li-yuqdiya Allahu amran kana maf'ula]...)

between life and death.

4. 11:44 (*...the matter <u>came to pass</u> [qudiya 'l-amr]...*) = meaning to be completed. Cf.6:60 (*that the term <u>specified for you</u> [li-yuqda] is fulfilled...*).

5. 43:77 (*...and they will cry, 'Lord! <u>Finish us off</u>!' [la-yuqdi 'alayna]...*) = meaning destroy us and make us perish.

- All the meanings for *qada'* as given in the Qur'an and the hadith refer to Allah's attributes (*sifat Allah*) as well as to His actions (*af'aluhu*). These terms are used in their *linguistic* sense and hence cannot be rationalised.

- If there is no *shar'i*-meaning discernible from the texts/sources (i.e. Qur'an and hadith), then a term that is given a technical definition cannot then be said to taken on a *shar'i*-meaning. Or, when there is only a linguistic meaning and no *shar'i*-meaning for a term, then it cannot then be arbitrarily given one.

- Regarding these verses, their subject-matter, study, discussion or investigation is *shar'i* but there meanings are linguistic (*lughawi*). The subject-matter, study, discussion or investigation of *al-qada' wa 'l-qadar* as defined by the *Mutakallimun* is rational ('*aqli*) and not textual. Thus, the discussion of *al-qada' wa 'l-qadar* is a technical term formulated by the Mutakallimun from a specific scholastic context. Neither the Companion nor the Successors designated a specific or technical definition for the terms *al-qada' wa 'l-qadar*. They were fully aware of the terms 'qada' and 'qadar' but **not** in the sense given to both of them by later scholastics/theologians.

- This specific or technical meaning given by later scholastics/theologians was introduced subsequent to the introduction of Greek thought and polemical encounters with neighbouring Christians and Jews.

References: For the word 'qadar', see s.v. "qaddara", J. Penrice, *A Dictionary and Glossary of the Qur'an*, pp.115-116 and al-Badawi and Haleem, *Arabic-English Dictionary of Qur'anic Usage*, s.v. "qadara", pp.740-742. For the word 'qada'', see s.v. "qada", J. Penrice, *A Dictionary and Glossary of the Qur'an*, p.118 and al-Badawi and Haleem, *Arabic-English Dictionary of Qur'anic Usage*, s.v. "qada", pp.763-764.

"Part 3:
al-Qada' wa 'l-Qadar Revisited"

Course: 'Early Islamic Controversies'
Topic: *qada' and qadar revisited*
Instructor: S. Z. Chowdhury
Venue: Ad-Duha Institute, London

- The *Mutakallimun* had designated a specific/technical meaning to the terms *qada'* and *qadar*, joining them together to give rise to the discussion that are now found in the books of *kalam*. This specific or technical meaning is nowhere to be found in the Qur'an, hadith or statements of the Sahabah because the discussion was based on a context lifted out of a inherited Hellenized background and lexicon.

- Indeed, there is a hadith that even has both terms combined as narrated by al-Bazzar from Jabir b. 'Abd Allah as follows:

"…after Allah's <u>decree and determination</u> of them…"[24]	…أكثر من يموت من <u>أمتي بعد قضاء الله وقدره في النفس</u>…

- However, this meaning in the hadith is not the same as what later *Mutakallimun* were to assign to it. Other *hadiths* also mention the terms but do not carry the specific/technical meaning assigned to it by later *Mutakallimun*:

"…protect me from the evil <u>you have decreed</u>…" – meaning guard and protect me from the evil you have ordained, decided and commanded.[25]	علمني رسول الله صلى الله عليه وسلم كلمات أقولهن في الوتر قال ابن جواس في قنوت الوتر: اللهم اهدني فيمن هديت وعافني فيمن عافيت وتولني فيمن توليت وبارك لي فيما أعطيت وقني شر ما قضيت إنك <u>تقضي ولا يقضى عليك</u> وإنه لا يذل من واليت ولا يعز من عاديت تباركت ربنا وتعاليت.

---

[24] The *isnad* ('chain of transmission') is *hasan* ('good') according Hafiz Ibn Hajar al-'Asqalani in *Fath al-Bari*, 10:211 & 214. See also Ibn 'Adi, *al-Kamil fi 'l-Du'afa'*, 5:191; al-Sakhawi, *al-Maqasid al-Hasanah*, p.349; al-Zarqani, *Mukhtasar al-Maqasid*, p.131 and al-'Ajluni, *Kashf al-Khafa'*, 2:99. And Allah knows best.

[25] A *hasan* (good) *hadith* as narrated by al-Tirmidhi and others in his *Sunan* (§1425) from al-Hasan b. 'Ali b. Abi Talib (may Allah be pleased with them).

"…to believe in *al-qada'* and *al-qadar* – the good and the bad…" – meaning to believe that Allah has ordained/written all things (whether they are good or evil) in the *lawh al-mahfuz*, meaning it is in the knowledge of Allah before they even come into existence.[26]

كان أول من قال في القدر بالبصرة معبد الجهني . فانطلقت أنا وحميد بن عبدالرحمن الحميري حاجين أو معتمرين فقلنا : لو لقينا أحد من أصحاب رسول الله صلى الله عليه وسلم فسألناه عما يقول هؤلاء في القدر . فوفق لنا عبدالله بن عمر بن الخطاب داخلا المسجد . فاكتنفته أنا وصاحبي . أحدنا عن يمينه والآخر عن شماله . فظننت أن صاحبي سيكل الكلام إلي . فقلت : أبا عبدالرحمن! إنه قد ظهر قبلنا ناس يقرؤون القرآن ويتقفرون العلم . وذكر من شأنهم وأنهم يزعمون أن لا قدر . وأن الأمر أنف . قال : فإذا لقيت أولئك فأخبرهم أني بريء منهم ، وأنهم براء مني . والذي يحلف به عبدالله بن عمر! لو أن لأحدهم مثل أحد ذهبا فأنفقه ، ما قبل الله منه حتى يؤمن بالقدر . ثم قال : حدثني أبي عمر بن الخطاب، قال :

بينما نحن عند رسول الله صلى الله عليه وسلم ذات يوم، إذ طلع علينا رجل شديد بياض الثياب . شديد سواد الشعر . لا يرى عليه أثر السفر . ولا يعرفه منا أحد . حتى جلس إلى النبي صلى الله عليه وسلم . فاسند ركبتيه إلى ركبتيه . ووضع كفيه على فخذيه . وقال : يا محمد ! أخبرني عن الإسلام . فقال رسول الله صلى الله عليه وسلم " : الإسلام أن تشهد أن لا إله إلا الله وأن محمدا رسول الله صلى الله عليه وسلم . وتقيم الصلاة . وتؤتي الزكاة . وتصوم رمضان . وتحج البيت، إن استطعت إليه سبيلا " قال : صدقت . قال فعجبنا له . يسأله ويصدقه . قال : فأخبرني عن الإيمان . قال : "أن تؤمن بالله، وملائكته، وكتبه ، ورسله ، واليوم الآخر . <u>وتؤمن بالقدر خيره وشره</u>" قال : صدقت . قال : فأخبرني عن الإحسان . قال : "أن تعبد الله كأنك تراه . فإن لم تكن تراه ، فإنه يراك" . قال : فأخبرني عن الساعة . قال : "ما المسؤول عنها بأعلم من السائل" قال : فأخبرني عن أماراتها . قال : "أن تلد الأمة ربتها . وأن ترى الحفاة العراة العالة رعاء الشاء ، يتطاولون في البنيان" . قال ثم انطلق . فلبثت مليا . ثم قال لي : "يا عمر !

---

[26] The narration with this wording is from the Muslim in his *Sahih* (§8).

أتدري من السائل ؟" قلت : الله ورسوله أعلم . قال " : فإنه جبريل أتاكم يعلمكم دينكم"...

- The Sahabah were aware of both the terms *qada'* and *qadar* but did not dispute the meanings. This was instigated by the inception of Greek thought and polemical encounter into the Muslim world at the close of the first century. The initial discussion of course centred around the emergence of the Qadariyyah sect.[27] They believed in the utter free will of human beings to the exclusion of diminishing Allah's power and knowledge.

- The meanings of the terms *qada'* and *qadar* as found in the verses of the Qur'an and hadith, therefore are restricted to their linguistic and *shar'i* (wherever found) meanings. Thus, the Qur'anic verses that mention Allah's knowledge (Omniscience) do not figure into the discussion of *al-qada' wa 'l-qadar*. Incorporating Allah's knowledge as well as the ontological nature of actions into the discussion of *al-qada' wa 'l-qadar* was a historical outcome and it produced three views that we have already discussed: the Mu'tazilah, Ash'ariyyah and the Jabriyyah.

- Neither were able to satisfactorily address the question due to the overarching context of the discussion which was inherited from the earlier discussions in antiquity.

- However, because the discussion was related to an essential pillar of the doctrine (*'aqidah*), it was necessary to address it.

References: See al-Nabhani, *al-Shakhsiyyah al-Islamiyyah*, 1:86-97. Much of the contents are repeated from the two earlier chapters. See also idem, *Nizam al-Islam*, ch.2. For general outlines of the topic, refer to the following entries in *The Encyclopaedia of the Qur'an* (ed. by J. McAuliffe): S. Schmidtke, "Destiny", 1:522, idem, "Determinism", 1:524; D. V. Frolov, "Freedom and Predestination", 2:267; W. Raven, "Reward and Punishment", 4:451; A. Karamustafa, "Fate", 2:185 and M. Radscheit, "Responsibility", 4:430. Cf. also, J. Van Ess, "Kadariyya" in EI^2, 4:368-372 and L. Gardet, "al-Kada wa-l-Kadar", in EI^2, 4:365-367.

---

[27] Not to be confused with the 'Qadiriyyah' Sufi *tariqah* of Shaykh 'Abd al-Qadir al-Jilani (may Allah have mercy on him). For more on the Qadariyyah sect, see

"Part 4: "al-Qada' wa 'l-Qadar: Some Conclusions"

Course: 'Early Islamic Controversies'
Topic: *qada' and qadar conclusions*
Instructor: S. Z. Chowdhury
Venue: Ad-Duha Institute, London

Context:

1. Early Muslim political events.
2. Qur'anic references to a strong/hard determinism (= antinomies of free will).
3. Encounters with Christian philosophical tradition in Iraq (8th century).
4. Entry of Hellenistic philosophy (Greek into Arabic movement).
5. Religious polemics.

Theological and Metaphysical basis

→Divine Fairness (beyond the sensible realm).
→Divine Omnipotence (beyond the sensible realm).
→Divine Omniscience (beyond the sensible realm).
→The ontological category of actions.
→Whether acts and their effects are created or not.

⇓

| This formed the basis and context for the discussion of *qada'* and *qadar*. |

Responses:

Four views arose from the early *kalam* discussions:

[1] The Qadariyyah = absolute free will;
[2] The Jabriyyah = absolute determinism;
[3] The Mu'tazilah = full libertarians;
[4] The Asha'irah = *kasb* theory.

All groups sought to uphold human moral freedom and accountability but with impact on how Divine character and attributes were to be understood. The topic was confounded more so by invoking Qur'anic verses o buttress each position in order to force the verses to take a philosophical it cannot bear.

- The basis of the discussion of *qada'* and *qadar* ought to be whether human beings actually have the *ikhtiyar* ('choice') to perform (or not perform) two opposite actions (one deemed bad and one deemed good). We can call this the "common sense" view.

- Human beings live in two 'domains' of existence. **One**: that domain in which h/she has the ability to choose between two actions (i.e. whether to do one or not). **Two**: that domain in which there is no influence or choice whatsoever and one is unable to act between two options. This domain in which there is no influence or choice whatsoever and one is unable to act between two options include:

a. Those actions that are part of the laws of the universe, e.g. the history of the world up until one is born; the laws of nature, etc.

b. Those that are not part of the laws of the universe but are nevertheless beyond anyone's control or choice but *enacted/performed* by human beings, e.g. a passenger on a train crash, s.o. falling off the wall onto somebody else, etc.

- Actions in this category of (a) and (b) is termed "qada'":

    a. Those that are pre-determined by Allah;
    b. Humans have no control over them;
    c. Humans will not be reckoned or judged for them.
    d. Human beings do not know whether or not they are beneficial or harmful.

- Free actions (*al-af'al al-ikhtiyariyyah*) do not fall under the term *qada'*.

- As for the term "qadar", it relates to objects in the universe. Actions are in relations with objects (action-objection *interface*). Allah created certain properties of objects, e.g. fire burns, knife cuts, etc. These properties are fixed and unalterable and obey the laws of nature. If these properties are altered, then it is a miraculous occurrence (*mu'jizah*). Included in this notion of *qadar* is the 'constitution' of a human being, i.e. what they are *made* of.

A Human being = intellect + [soul] + body {*instincts* [of survival, procreation, religiosity] and *natural needs* [of eating, drinking, breathing]}.

- These are ordained properties by Allah. Human beings may satisfy these needs and instincts in a way that accords with the standard of the law (*shar'*) or not. If the action utilizes an attribute of an object that satisfies the standard of the law then it is termed a praiseworthy/good action. If the action utilizes an attribute of an object that **does not** satisfy the standard of the law then it is termed a blameworthy/bad action.

- Note:

    a. All actions of the domain in which there is no influence or choice whatsoever and one is unable to act between two options whether good or bad, is from Allah.
    b. All properties (including the 'constitution' of a human being, i.e. what they are *made* of) whether resulting in good or bad is from Allah.
    c. Thus, *qada'* – good or bad – is from Allah.
    d. The *qadar* – good or bad and all it entails – is also from Allah.

- The domain in which h/she has the ability to choose between two actions (i.e. whether to do one or not) is the domain wherefrom judgment and reckoning will take place.

- Although attributes are (pre)determined by Allah, their *potential* for good/benefit and bad/harm is freely unlocked by human beings, e.g. a knife has the property to cut but a person has the free choice to either stab someone with it or not. Objects with their properties in the universe do not *compel* a person to act, e.g. a knife does not *force* a person to commit an act of murder.

- If a person freely carries out an action that accord with the standards of the law, then it is considered good, correct and right. If a person freely carries out an action that does not accord with the standards of the law, then it is considered bad, incorrect and wrong.

"Part 5: al-Ash'ari's Theory of *Kasb* ('Acquisition')"

Course: 'Early Islamic Controversies'
Topic: *Ashari and kasb*
Instructor: S. Z. Chowdhury
Venue: Ad-Duha Institute, London

Before al-Ash'ari formulated his theory on reconciling human agency with Divine Omnipotence, there were Mu'tazilite thinkers who had already begun discussing how to accommodate free will with Allah's Power in terms of not creating one's actions but 'acquiring' it – the Arabic term being *kasb* (كسب). A number of Qur'anic texts were also cited as evidences to support the idea that humans acquire their actions, i.e. they gain it through themselves but only because Allah creates the capacity within them to acquire it (cf. Q. 4:112; 52:16). Thus, Allah creates all things including actions but human beings possess them or appropriate them through their own efforts.

Below is an outline of the theory of *Kasb* from al-Ash'ari's *Kitab al-Luma'*, pars.82-164 (cf. also Frank, "The Structure of Created Causality According to al-Aš'ari", pp.17-35; Watt, *The Formative Period of Islamic Thought*, pp.199-201; Wolfson, *The Philosophy of the Kalam*, pp.663-719; Schwarz, "Acquisition (*kasb*) in Early Kalam", pp.373-377 and Abrahamov, "A Re-Examination of al-Ash'ari's Theory of *Kasb*", pp.210-220). It is important to bear in mind the following points regarding the background to al-Ash'ari's theory of *kasb*:

1. al-Ash'ari's theory of *kasb* is not novel (see below with the comparison with al-Najjar's formulation of it).

2. al-Ash'ari's doctrine is less concerned with human responsibility than with Divine Omnipotence (the former he takes as given but the latter can never be compromised or diminished).

3. His formulation of *kasb* is in the context of a polemical exchange with his Mu'tazilite adversaries.

4. Atoms (*jawahir*) and accidents (*a'rad*) form the metaphysical backdrop of *kasb*.

5. He has considerations that are *epistemological* (how do we know we are free?), *ontological* (what are the status of physical actions in reality?) and *phenomenological* (are we conscious that we are free?).

The Doctrine of *Kasb*:

Husayn al-Najjar

See al-Ash'ari's reports in *al-Maqalat al-Islamiyyin*, pp.283-285 and 567:

وقال ((النجّار)): إن الإنسان قادر على الكسب، عاجز عن الخلق، وإن المقدور على كسبه هو المعجوز عن خلقه

"al-Najjar held the view that human beings are able to acquire their actions but unable to create it; thus what is possible is acquiring the act but not creating it […]"

أن أعمال العباد مخلوقة لله، وهم فاعلون لها ... وأن الاستطاعة لا يجوز أن تتقدّم الفعل، وأن العون من الله سبحانه يحدث في حال الفعل مع الفعل وهو الاستطاعة، وأن الاستطاعة الواحدة لا يُفعل بها فعلان، وإن لكل فعل استطاعة تحدث معه إذا حدث. وأن الاستطاعة لا تبقى، وأن في وجودها وجود الفعل، وفي عدمها عدم الفعل، وإن استطاعة الإيمان توفيق وتسديد، وفضل ونعمة وإحسان وهُدئً، وإن استطاعة الكفر ضلال وخذلان وبلاءٌ وشرٌّ، وأنه جائز كون الطاعة في حال المعصية التي هي تركها بأن لا تكون كانت المعصية التي تركها في ذلك الوقت، وبأن لا يكون كان الوقت وقتاً للمعصية التي هي تركها.

"[…] that the actions of human beings are created by Allah but they are agents of it […] and that the capacity to act (*istita'ah*) cannot precede the act itself and that the assistance from from Allah (glorified is He!) is created or originated at the time of the act *with* the act and this is the capacity; the capacity to act is singular and no two acts may be produced from the one capacity and that for every act a capacity is created simultaneously with it when the act is carried out. The capacity to

al-Ash'ari

See "The Theory of *Kasb* According to al-Ashari" at http://daralnicosia.wordpress.com/2011/05/19/the-doctrine-of-kasb-according-to-al-ashari/

1. *Qudrah* = 'power', 'ability'.
2. *Fa'il* = 'agent', 'doer'.
3. *Istita'ah* = 'capacity'.
4. *Kasb* = 'acquisition'.
5. *Fi'l* = 'act'.
6. *Quwwah* = 'strength', 'ability'.

From al-Ash'ari's view we have the following formulation:

1. Allah in reality creates action A of S.
2. For every action A there is required a created power, p through which A is executed.
3. For every action A there is required a capacity, c enabling A to be executed.
4. No A can be executed without p.
5. No A can be executed without c.
6. At time t_1 S desires to carry out A where Allah creates the capacity, c and power, p to carry out A <u>simultaneously</u> with A.
7. S acquires the capacity and power externally (i.e. from Allah) to carry out A.

act does not endure and the act exists with its existence and does not exist in its absence […]"

From al-Najjar's view we have the following formulation:

1. Allah creates action A of S.
2. For every action A there is its unique and singular concomitant capacity, c for A to be executed.
3. No A can be carried out without c.
4. At time t_1 S desires to carry out A where Allah creates its capacity, c to carry out A <u>simultaneously</u> with A.
5. S acquires the capacity extrinsically (i.e. from Allah) to carry out A.
6. At another time t_2, a new capacity, c^* is created for A that is not identical to the previous capacity, c related to its act.

[End].

S. Z. Chowdhury.
London, 2012.
(updated)

Basic Bibliography

- B. Abrahamov, "Theology" in *The Blackwell Companion to the Qur'an*, ed. by A. Rippin, pp.420-435.

  ——— *Islamic Theology: Traditionalism and Rationaalism.*

- M. Abdel Haleem, "Early Kalam", pp.71-88 and J. Pavlin, "Sunni Kalam", pp.105-118 both in *History of Islamic Philosophy*, ed. O. Leaman and S. H. Nasr.

- K. Blankenship, "The Early Creed", pp.pp.33-54; O. Leaman and S. Rizvi, "The Developed *Kalam* Tradition", pp.77-96 and "God: Essence and Attributes", pp.121-140 all in *The Cambridge Companion to Classical Islamic Theology*, ed. by T. Winter.

- F. A. Klein, *The Religion of Islam*, pp.37-106.

- F. E. Peters, *Aristotle and The Arabs*, pp.135-220.

- M. M. Sharif, ed. *A History of Muslim Philosophy*, 2 vols; vol.1, ch.7-15.

- D. Waines, *An Introduction to Islam*, pp.103-132.

- W. M. Watt, *The Formative Period of Islamic Thought*.

  ——— *Islamic Philosophy and Theology.*

- A. J. Wensinck. *The Muslim Creed*, 58-82 and 248-276.

- H. A. Wolfson, *The Philosophy of the Kalam*, pp.1-57.

Notes

Printed in Great Britain
by Amazon